ExPLORING in the NEXT WORLD

by Jack MacArthur

Foreword by Louis T. Talbot, D.D.

DIMENSION BOOKS
BETHANY FELLOWSHIP, INC.
Minneapolis, Minnesota

Grateful acknowledgment is made to the following for permission to use copyrighted material:

Fleming H. Revell Company, for quotation from *Man Does Not Stand Alone* by A. Cressy Morrison.

Wm. B. Eerdmans Publishing Company, for material from *Evidences of Immortality* by Harry Rimmer.

The MacMillan Company, for quotation from *The Problem of Pain* by C. S. Lewis.

Printed in the United States of America

CONTENTS

FOREWORD

I am honored to recommend unreservedly and enthusiastically this fine treatment of a subject near to the heart of all people by my long-time friend, Dr. Jack MacArthur. Covering as it does the matter of life after death, this volume is most timely since statistics show that the rise of interest in spiritism is greater than it has been for several decades. In *Exploring in the Next World*, Dr. MacArthur deals with many aspects of the life to come, including the question of communication with the dead and the reality of heaven. He corroborates his statements with Scripture and enhances them with telling illustrations. The book is concise, authoritative, moving, and readable, and for it I predict a wide circulation.

I have deepest respect for Dr. MacArthur's long, faithful and effective ministry in the pulpit, on radio and TV, and in Christian literature, and I hold him in highest esteem and affection as a personal friend and co-worker in the vineyard of the Lord.

Louis T. Talbot, D.D.
Chancellor of Biola College and
Talbot Theological Seminary

chapter one

WHAT IS DEATH?

*"For the living know that they shall die . . ." (Eccles.
9:5).*

"It is appointed unto men once to die, but after this
the judgment" (Heb. 9:27).

Death is a fact. Forty million people die every year;
109,589 a day; 4,566 an hour; 76 a minute. Death
comes equally to us all and makes us all equal when it
comes.

> *The prince who kept the world in awe,*
> *The judge whose dictate fixed the law,*
> *The rich, the poor, the great, the small,*
> *All leveled, death confounds them all.*

There is no arguing the fact of death. For, as William
Cullen Bryant says in *Thanatopsis:* "All that tread the
globe are but a handful to the tribes that slumber in its
bosom. Take the wings of the morning, pierce the Bar-
can wilderness, or lose thyself in the continuous woods
where rose the oregon, and hear no sounds save his own
dashings, yet, the dead are there. Millions in those soli-
tudes, since first the flight of years began, have laid them
down in their last sleep . . ." And now, on Long Island,
the body of the man who wrote those exquisite lines

sleeps with the millions in death's solitude.

But what is death? One has written:

> 'Tis slumber to the weary,
> 'Tis rest to the forlorn,
> 'Tis shelter to the dreary,
> 'Tis peace amid the storm,
> 'Tis the entrance to our home,
> 'Tis the passage to that God
> **Who bids His children come,**
> When this weary course is trod.

However, no passage of prose can remove the natural antipathy that the normal man has for death.

It is quite unnatural to welcome death. God created man to live and not to die. God's will for us all is that we should live well and long, as long as we can, and as well as we can, by His grace.

> There is no flock,
> However watched and tended,
> But one dead lamb is there,
> There is no fireside
> Howsoe'er defended,
> But has one vacant chair.

How many times we have wondered about death. All of us, in the course of life, have been at some time, whether we know it or not, at the gate of death. We wonder how it will feel when our eyes are open but do not see, when our ears are receptive but do not hear, when our arms and our limbs, still filled with blood, have no ability to move themselves. Inch by inch the body grows still and breathing gets more difficult. The body becomes lifeless and at last, those who are near, say, "He is dead," or "She is dead."

2

Job said, "Man dieth . . . and where is he?" Surely death is an adventure. What happens to the soul when it leaves the body and starts out into the great hereafter? To the millions who have died, to the millions who now live, and to the millions who shall live, this is an important question. If the Lord delays His return, all of us will make this journey. We may be called upon at any moment to make this pilgrimage, this great adventure, into the land of death, for "Who knoweth the day of his death?" In the midst of life we are in death. "How far is it to the grave?" Not very far for any of us. Every step we have taken from birth has been in the direction of the grave. The Holy Book says that our days are like a hand's breadth, and life is like a vapor that appears for a moment and then is gone. "They are like grass . . . In the morning it flourisheth . . . in the evening it is cut down, and withereth" (Psalm 90:5,6).

The generations of men chase each other in rapid succession as shadows o'er the plain and continue not. On the train, in the automobile, on the sea, in the air, on the land, by your fireside, at your desk, anywhere you may be, the call may come to you to make that journey. It is inevitable; it is certain. "It is appointed unto men once to die . . ." (Heb. 9:27). This is man's destined end. None can escape.

Someone has said:

> The king must lay aside his crown, step down from his throne and lie down beside the beggar in the clods of the valley. The minister must pronounce his final benediction, close his Bible and surrender his flock to the Great Shepherd of the sheep. The magistrate must change his judicial ermine for garments of the sepulchre. The lawyer must write his last brief and finish his final legation. The author, his last col-

3

umn, the poet, his final verse. The actor must play his last scene and leave the stage forever. The laborer must leave his plow in the field, his ax in the woodland and give his brawny, stalwart frame to the grave. The soldier must march for the last time and pay the supreme price for liberty in the grim ordeal of war. The mother must leave her chair tenantless and her helpless babies alone. The innocent, playful child must drop his toys and with his tiny arms grapple with death.

The time of this event is uncertain, but the fact of it is as certain and sure as that we now live.

Death is full of mystery. It is a silent, unsurveyed land into which no philosopher or scientist has ever forced his way. One philosopher said, "Every avenue of approach seems darkened by impenetrable shadow. No man by searching can find it out."

After all, what death is depends upon what life is, and what a mysterious thing life is. Its Inventor needs no patent because no one else knows how to make it. Its mysterious quality eludes us. The great Queen of England offered worlds for more life, but all the millions of the British Empire could not buy a single second more of time.

What is life? No man has yet satisfactorily answered the question. Reason has yet to solve life's riddle. Science has yet to explain life's reason. Only if you were able to reduce God to the component parts of a laboratory demonstration would this problem be solved. Perhaps it has never occurred to you that life, which we cannot explain but which unmistakably is, must be accepted by faith. Inevitably life, until you deliberately, finally deny it, until you destroy it, strengthens faith. About all we can do is describe life. Spencer defines physical life for us as correspondence with environment.

Birth is as great a mystery as death. An artist completed a beautiful statue and invited his friend to see it. His friend, although enraptured in the beauty of the masterpiece, said, "Something is wrong. There is one thing missing!" The artist inquired what was wrong, what was missing. He answered, "There is no life." The artist could make the form of a man to such an exactness that it was almost startling but he could not make it breathe; he could not make it grow; he could not impart to it that elusive thing called life.

To be alive means to be in active, vital correspondence with the environment present. For example, the environment of the eye is light; the environment of the ear is sound. But when the whole organism collapses—the lungs refuse to correspond with their environment, air; and the heart refuses to correspond with its environment, blood, — we say a thing is dead. That explanation, from a physical standpoint, is perhaps as good as can be made; but surely this is not all there is in life and in death.

Is it not true that both life and death, in their real significance, depend upon what man is? And what a mystery man is! When we think of man, it is not his physical outline or the body in which he appears, or the color of his eyes, or his hair; but it is the intangible something that animates him, that is the *real* man. The most sublime fact of human life is the fact of personality, the fact of *you* — not your eyes, your hands, your voice but *you,* that which we miss when you are gone, even for a little while.

What, then, is gone at death? All the organs may be present within the body but the heart has stopped beating and all the functions have ceased. What is missing? The elusive part that really is the man is the part that is missing — whatever that is which animates the body.

What is it then, that makes the man? An analytical authority tells us that the constituent parts of a man would be equal to about 1200 eggs, iron to make 2 ten-penny nails, phosphorus to make 4,000 matches, fat to make 75 candles and one cake of soap, enough hydrogen to fill a balloon and carry it above the clouds, about 60 spoonfuls of salt, a bowl of sugar, and about six gallons of water.

Dr. Charles Mayo of the Mayo Clinic in Rochester, Minnesota, said, "Enough lime to whitewash a chicken coop, magnesium enough to make a dose of magnesia, potassium enough to explode a toy cannon, and sulphur enough to rid a dog of fleas. The total value would be about ninety-nine cents."

But is that all there is to a man? To ask the question is to answer it, for man is vastly more than his chemical constituency. The most convincing human reason for belief in immortality is personality.

It has been well said:

Science comes from the dissecting room, scalpel in hand, to report its failure to find anything in the human organism bearing the stamp of immortality. But we affirm immortality as that which we call spirit, that which no scalpel has ever laid open, that which no lens has ever enabled the eyes to see, that to which belong none of the known properties of matter, and which is, nevertheless, sovereign over matter. That which thinks, reasons, plans, wills, loves, fears, suffers and enjoys. That which, reaching out into the realm of nature, subdues and shapes it to its own higher purposes. That which, using the marvelous mechanism of the body, sees, hears, and feels. It is the man who has brain, sense, muscle, but of whom brain, sense, and muscle form no permanent part. It is the man who works through a physical mechanism but who is no more to be confounded with the mechanism than the mallet and the chisel are to be confounded with the sculptor. This body is a material agent, but I am a soul.

The soul is the immaterial substance, inaccessible to all violence from matter and therefore cannot perish with the body. The soul is the perpendicular "I" that we speak about so much and think about even more. It cannot be the body, for the body is only the temporary house in which the "I" lives. The body changes in appearance daily and hourly from birth. It completely changes, so science tells us, approximately every seven years. A man of forty-nine has actually had seven bodies, yet the same "I" lives in it. If the mind were material — if it were of the body — it would have undergone a corresponding change; therefore, every seven years a man's consciousness that he *is* would have changed. There could not be any recollection of his past life, or knowledge of personal identity, or assurance that at forty-nine years of age he is the same person he was at 21 or 35. You know you have undergone changes, yet you have the consciousness of personal identity.

What is that something which has remained intact, that has not been affected by the perpetual replacement of old material by new? In our human microorganism, every time the watch ticks, there are millions of molecules of the old body dissolved and carried away, and their place is filled by as many millions of new. Yet you know, notwithstanding this process of destruction going on in every portion of your frame, that throughout the years you have maintained your personal identity. This fact forces you to admit the presence of something besides matter, something that is free from the perpetual changes to which matter is subject. Matter passes on, while the spiritual substance called soul endures, distinct from and independent to matter. The body may die and the brain may die but the "I" lives on. "I *am* a soul; I *live* in a body."

The scientific world makes the assertion that the brain is only an instrument. A symphony cannot be played without instruments. It is the Beethoven behind the instrument that makes music. The mechanical apparatus is the instrument through which he produces the wonderful harmony. The brain and the body are only the instruments through which the man reveals himself and makes the music of life. The mysterious "I" is behind the brain, using it and even educating it. The brain may be the seat of your thinking but never the source of it. We are always using it and molding it for our own purposes. It is never the origin of anything. The question concerning the dependence of the mind upon the brain can have no necessary relation to the question of our future life.

Physiology and psychology are both coming to the conviction that the brain is not the maker but the instrument of personality. The person uses the brain to serve his will, but only a small quantity of this substance. In this present life the mind may be dependent upon the brain but that does not necessarily say it must always be dependent upon that instrument for its existence or usefulness.

The worm in the cocoon or the bird in the egg lives in that special environment and is dependent upon it for life, but the relation is not permanent. It will someday be outgrown and a new environment will make for a larger and better life.

If the brain does not create the mind, then the physical structure is not the condition upon which the invisible self depends. A man uses his eyes but he is a man, and sometimes a better man, without them. A man can never see without the visual lobe of the brain; but that special bundle of nerves is not the man. We may be dependent upon the instruments we use but they are not our creators. The musician may use an instrument to reveal his symphony to his fellow men, but he can throw away the instruments and he himself is still the amazing symphony.

It would be a greater mystery if we said the brain created personality. It is far more thinkable and understandable to say the brain is the instrument used by the human soul. How could a mass of protoplasm compose a sermon? Personality uses the fiber, blood, tissue, cells and nerves. Thus, I am assured I am a permanent, mysterious, unchanging, spiritual being with an ever-changing body and brain. If my body is changing constantly and yet I remain the same, it is certain I will survive the passing of my whole body at death. It bursts upon me like a great light that I live in a body, but I am a soul.

Jesus placed a tremendous value upon the soul when He declared: "For what shall it profit a man, if he shall gain the whole world, and lose his own soul? Or what shall a man give in exchange for his soul?" (Mark 8:36, 37). When I give that which is the essential me — my soul — to God, in the consciousness of my sin and my need, and the precious blood of Christ becomes the antitoxin to cleanse my soul, taking away the disease, the guilt, and the consequences of sin, which is ultimately eternal death, I am brought into a vital union with Jesus

Christ. I know I have the promise that when the sun is ashes and the stars have gone out forever, I shall be but beginning my eternal life with Christ. That life will be untrammeled, unhindered, forever and forever, world without end — because I am a soul. I live only temporarily in a body.

Socrates made the statement, "You catch my body, but you cannot catch my soul, myself, to bury me." Where did he get that? He had no Bible. It was a revelation of the self that was within him.

Human reason, logic, scientific evidence and philosophy unite in saying that man is a thing apart from his body. Man is a soul and that soul will live on after the death of the body. It will live in one of two worlds — a world with God or a world without God. The Scripture recognizes the distinction between the body and the spiritual nature of man: "But there is a spirit in man: and the inspiration of the Almighty giveth them understanding" (Job 32:8). "The Lord . . . stretcheth forth the heavens, and layeth the foundation of the earth, and formeth the spirit of man within him" (Zech. 12:1).

Divine revelation, then, corroborates the testimony of human reason. The spirit of man and the body of man are as distinct as the house and the tenant who dwells there. "For ye are bought with a price; therefore glorify God in your body, and in your spirit, which are God's" (I Cor. 6:20). "For what man knoweth the things of a man, save the spirit of a man which is in him?" (I Cor. 2:11).

We have the clear teaching of the Lord Jesus Christ that men may kill the body but they cannot kill the soul. In Matt. 10:28 He said, "And fear not them which kill the body, but are not able to kill the soul."

The history of creation shows man to be a compound being. Note the order of events as outlined in Gen. 2:7:

1. God "formed man out of the dust of the ground." Man had no consciousness, no life, no motion, no sensation, no ability to correspond with his environment. There was only the "form" of man.
2. "God breathed into his nostrils the breath of life" or, as it is in the Hebrew, "the living spirit," and man became a living soul and entered into immediate correspondence with the environment that surrounded him.

Conversely, when a person dies, the brain, the eyes, the ears, and the nerves are still the same members that were present before. Yet, in death, the brain cannot think, the eyes cannot see, the ears cannot hear and the nerves produce no feeling, because it was not the body but the real spiritual nature within the body that did the thinking, the seeing, the hearing and the feeling. The living spirit has been withdrawn.

Dr. Charles Mayo said, "The keen blade of my scalpel may never uncover the soul as a tangible part of the mystery called man, but I know it is there. I am as confident of its presence as I am of the most elemental truth to which my medical science adheres." God's word says unmistakably and repeatedly that man has, that man is a soul.

Forms may change but life itself moves with a tide as irresistible as the recurring seasons. Reason tells us to apply this same principle to our personality. Personality may change its residence and lay aside the flesh that clothed it, but it is never destroyed. What we call "death" does not involve extinction, only change.

According to the positive teaching of the most advanced science of the day, nothing in the whole realm of nature is really destroyed in the sense of being annihilated. We have no power over matter to destroy it — we can only change its form. You may freeze a drop of water, heat it to steam, decompose it into its elementary gases, or explode it — it still exists — every atom of it. Dispense or change its elements as you may, they will forever defy all efforts to annihilate them. Annihilation is a name for that which has never yet occurred and never can, much less for that which is immaterial—man's soul. It is an established law of nature that nothing that is once launched into being ever goes out of existence. The word destruction never means annihilation, for nothing is ever annihilated. When you destroy something you render it unfit to fulfill the purpose for which it was made. "The wicked shall be punished with everlasting destruction." They will never fulfill the purpose for which they were created, but they will not be annihilated.

Death, in the Word of God, always means one thing: separation. Physical death is the separation of the soul from the body. "Dust thou art, and unto dust shalt thou return" (Gen. 3:19). "Wherefore, as by one man sin entered into the world, and death by sin; and so death passed upon all men, for that all have sinned" (Rom. 5:12).

The phrase, "death passed upon all men," according to Thayer, means: "No one being able to stop it or to escape its power."

Adam enjoyed intimate, glorious, wonderful fellowship

with God. But God warned him that in the day he sinned he would die. Adam had never seen anybody die; but when he sinned, that day he died. What happened? He did not immediately die physically, but the moment he was out of correspondence with his former spiritual environment, he lost his relationship with God; and when he heard the voice of God he ran and hid himself. He had lost communion with God. Spiritually, he died immediately; physically he *began* to die. The sentence of physical death was carried out all the days of Adam's earthly life. It was finally fully executed in the separation of his soul from his body.

Spiritual death is the separation of the soul from God. "And you hath he quickened, who were dead (slain) in trespasses and sins" (Eph. 2:1). "But God . . . even when we were dead in sins, hath quickened us together with Christ" (Eph. 2:5). "To be carnally minded is death; but to be spiritually minded is life and peace" (Romans 8:6). The Apostle wrote to Timothy: "She that liveth in pleasure is dead while she liveth" (I Tim. 5:6).

Spiritual death is not "eternal death." Eternal death or eternal separation from God is the final state of the godless, unregenerate soul. Eternal death comes only when physical death takes place before the spirit, which is dead in trespasses and sin, is made alive by the regeneration of the Holy Spirit. What eternal death means to the soul no one can fully know until he finds himself ushered into its ghastly experience. "The fearful, and unbelieving . . . shall have their part in the lake which burneth with fire and brimstone: which is the second death" (Rev. 21:8).

Why will men die? As physical life is correspondence with a physical environment, spiritual life is correspondence with spiritual reality; and not to be related to a spiritual environment is spiritual death. Man is the most alive of all living things. A stone has an environment but an extremely limited correspondence with it. A tree responds to nature's environment but man corresponds with a more vast environment. He seems to correspond with the whole realm that surrounds him.

However, there is another sphere beyond this which the natural man does not understand. Man in general is a stranger to it and the reason is that he is dead spiritually. Give this environment a name; call it God and change the word correspondence to communion and it is exactly the concept, the state, the condition that the Word of God describes as spiritual life. Its opposite is spiritual death. For the unbeliever, death is separation from God forever. The Scripture says, "When a wicked man dieth, his expectation shall perish . . . (Proverbs 11:7).

Hobbs, the infidel, when he was dying, said, "I am taking a fearful leap into the dark." Charles IX proclaimed in the hour of his death: "I know not where I am; I am lost forever, I know."

The Scripture speaks of the unbeliever as being without God and without hope. For him physical death is the terror of terrors, because it ultimately means eternal death, with nothing but hopelessness and despair forever. It is impenetrable darkness, a leap into the unknown, where the soul is utterly lost and forever doomed. The Scripture describes that final state of separation that severs the soul from the life of God forever, as "the second death" (Rev. 2:18).

What a different aspect physical death has for the believer. Instead of the end, it is the beginning. Speaking from a physical point of view, what appears to be death is not death at all. The difficulty with most in thinking of the future life, is that of appearances, which can be deceptive and misleading. The least of all reality is found in appearances. A seed appears dead but it is not. The sun appears to rise in the east and set in the west but it does not. To all appearances the earth is flat but it is not. The leaves fall off the trees in autumn and in all appearances the tree is dead; but with the coming of spring it bursts with new foliage as it clothes itself with the glory of that hidden life. The earth appears to stand still but it does not.

Appearances deceive and create doubts about life after death. The dead body says, "This is the end," and we might be foolish enough to believe this illusion, but the appearance is most deceptive. The conscious personality in Christ still lives and belongs to that body only in the sense that a tenant belongs to a house. The Christian who closes his eyes in death is already opening them in a fuller, more glorious, abundant life. For the Christian, death is simply a transition into the highest possible life. It is natural to shrink from death if we do not have the Christian's faith and hope. Then why should we, who are believers, be afraid of death?

Imagine Adam and Eve on their first day upon the earth. As the day closed there shone above the greater glories of a new and more wonderful world which the light of day had hidden. So it is with death for the believer. Small wonder that D. L. Moody shouted, "Earth is receding, heaven is opening and God is calling." To the Christian death is the robing room where he prepares himself for going in to see the King in all His beauty. It is a walk through the valley of the shadow with the

Saviour's hand in his until the light breaks and he sees Him face to face. "Eye hath not seen, nor ear heard, neither have entered into the heart of man, the things which God hath prepared for them that love him" (I Cor. 2:9).

The father of H. S. Laird lay dying. His son went to his bedside and asked, "Dad, how do you feel about the whole experience?" The great saint, in the ecstasy of the consciousness of Christ's presence, and looking forward to the glories that were to be his in the world to come, turned his face toward his young minister son and replied: "Son, I feel like a little boy on Christmas Eve."

How enrapturing is the thought that death has forever lost its sting in Christ. "O death, where is thy sting? O grave, where is thy victory? . . . But thanks be to God which giveth us the victory through our Lord Jesus Christ" (I Cor. 15:55, 57).

chapter two

YOU WILL SURVIVE DEATH

"If a man die, shall he live again?" (Job 14:14).

No question can more seriously engage the attention of man than the one contained in the above Scripture. To the millions who now live and shall live after we are gone, this is indeed an important question. All through history this interrogation has forced its way up from the depths of every human soul. This question Job asked is as old as the history of man.

From the world's earliest morning, the thoughts of man linked life to a longer chain of time than that between birth and death. Every arch built in religion's name has had immortality as its keystone. Buddhists, Mohammedans, cultists, Christians, agnostics, infidels, men of every faith, men who say they have no faith at all, will engage in discussions on this question, "Are the dead alive?" Do we survive the chemical change called death?"

It makes all the difference of both worlds to me whether my life is ephemeral, a candle suddenly snuffed out, a gleam of consciousness between the cradle and the grave, or whether in me there is something that is going to survive the limitations of time, space and the corruption of matter; whether this life is the palace of existence, or whether, as Browning said, it is but "the vestibule of the palace."

There are two answers to Job's great question, (1) The answer of human reason, which we shall consider in this section. (2) The answer of divine revelation, with which we shall deal later on. These two testimonies, in marvelous harmony, corroborate to tell us that man does live on beyond the grave. As we have seen, it is the man who works through the physical mechanism. This is the permanent entity that really is the man that we believe lives after death.

To repeat, the brain does not think, will, or remember. The human brain on the dissecting table is a mere mass of cells and nerve centers suffused with blood. The best modern science asserts that "I" am a mysterious, unchanging, spiritual being behind this ever-changing brain. The brain is an instrument, nothing more. "I" decide what goes into that brain as a memory. "I" decide how that instrument is going to be used. But what is that "I"?

An eminent scientist recently said that no one knows where the mind is, and it is the mind that uses the brain. He should be told that what he is talking about is the soul of man, the intangible part of man that is the man. The violinist cannot produce violin music without a violin, but he is just as much a musician without it. The brain may be the seat of thought, but it is certainly not the source of thought.

The brain of a baboon differs very little from the brain of a man. The difference is in the being who is behind it— the one who is using it. A great scientist said, "As far as I can see, if the soul of a man can get behind the brain of an ape, he could probably use it almost as well as his own." "But there is a spirit in man: and the inspiration of the Almighty giveth them understanding" (Job 32:8). "But there is a vital force, a spirit of intelligence in man, and the breath of the Almighty gives men understanding" (Amp.). An ape does not possess that "vital force," that "spirit of intelligence."

Dr. Gustav Stromberg, famous astronomer and author, says in his book, *The Soul of the Universe,* that in the non-physical world lies the fountainhead of life. Our consciousness is rooted in a world not built of atoms. It has been discovered that organizing, living electrical fields seem to emerge from 'another world" into the physical world, organizing and planning the development of life. This we see in our microscopes and investigate in our laboratories. There are strong reasons to believe that at death they disappear into the world from which they originally came.

In recent years extensive studies have been made of these organizing fields. The section of neuro-anatomy at Yale Medical School has been particularly active in this research. All living organisms are imbedded in complex electric fields, and these fields disappear at death. Dr. H. S. Burr, leader of the research group at Yale, states it is hard to escape the conclusion that these fields are independent of the matter involved and by their innate properties determine the structure and functions of the living organism.

All our mental characteristics and faculties have their origin in the non-physical world. There lies the origin of our sensations of light, color, sound, and music. Here is the origin of our feelings and emotions, our will and thoughts. This is the source of satisfaction and bliss, of guilt and remorse. Our nerve cells seem to be the links that connect our physical brain with the world in which our consciousness is rooted. At death our brain field, which during our life determined the structure and functions of our brain and nervous system, is not destroyed. Like other living fields, it contracts and disappears at death. All of our memories are indelibly engraved in this field; and after our death, when our mind is no longer blocked by inert matter, we can probably recall them all, even those of which we were never consciously aware during our organic life.

In other words, these researchers at the Yale Medical School discovered there is a force that supervises the development of the embryo and the fetus. As that force exerts itself, the body begins to take form according to the direction received. As a person develops and grows, the electrical field becomes increasingly complicated with the development of the brain.

Then an amazing thing was discovered. When a person dies, instead of a gradual process, scientists have discovered that this complicated mechanism leaves the body suddenly—not a little at a time. In the experience of death, there is a moment when the entire complex electrical structure leaves all at once, and can be measured in leaving. That is why Einstein said this is the most powerful argument for immortality that he had ever heard in all of his life. From the argument of this eminent scientist, the body actually limits and confines the soul. "It doth not yet appear what we shall be: but we know that, when he shall appear, we shall be like him; for we shall see him as he is" (I John 3:2). I live in a body, but

I myself am a soul. This is the being we believe will live after death; that is, the man that will outlive the wreck of his mortal body and will "live again."

From the point of view of reason, we argue that there is a future life because this is a universal belief, desire and hope. You could burn every Bible, blot out and erase every vestige of Scripture from the hearts of men and they would still believe in existence after death, for it is a God-given instinct.

In all the history of ethnology there has never been a race without this hope. The Egyptians believed in a future life 3,000 years before the feet of Jesus pressed the Galilean hills. They prepared the bodies of their dead with great care and expense, for they felt this life was not all. Plato, Aristotle, and Socrates, in their philosophies, reveal the same longing for, and belief in, immortality. Democritus said, "The soul is the house of God." Virgil, Ovid, and Homer taught the truth of immortality in their poetry. Homer, nine hundred years before Christ, taught that the present life is but a shadow of the future life. We find this sentiment not only among the cultured nations, but diffused throughout the islands of the Pacific, and over Lapland, Asia, and Africa. Our American Indians believed that far beyond the distant blue there was an expanse of water, full of laughing, blooming islands with spacious hunting grounds, where they would go after death. This instinct, desire, and longing for life after death is very deep in the subconscious nature of man. It is intuitive.

Since man possesses an "instinct for eternity," there must be an eternity to answer the longing. The intuitiveness of a hereafter is the counterpart of reality, even as the reflection of a face in the water is sufficient evidence that the face itself is not an illusion. The idea of immortality is interwoven in the mind and is part of the soul's original furniture. It is God's appointed witness that we shall live again; therefore immortality must be the end to which it leads. If man has an instinct looking forward to a future life and there is no future life provided for him, then he is the solitary exception to an otherwise universal rule.

There is no example in nature of an organic instinct without its correlate. Nature never utters false prophecies. There is food for hunger, water for thirst, light for the eye, sound for the ear, problems for intelligence, and love for the object of devotion. This is true in all of nature, even as there is air for the wings of a bird. If this be true in regard to the impulses of physical life, why should it not be true with the superior instincts of the soul. There must be a hereafter to answer man's longing and hope.

In the deepening twilight of a summer evening a pastor called on one of his parishioners, a little blind lad, and found him flying a kite. The pastor, seeing the kite high in the sky, remarked, "Jimmie, lad, I can see your kite in the sky; you can't see it, so how do you know it's there?"

The little fellow turned his sightless eyes toward his pastor and said, "Pastor, I cannot see it but I know it's there, because I feel the tug and the pull of this string that I hold in my hand." So it is that man, by instinct, feels the tug and the pull of the life beyond.

The Scripture speaks of the fact that God has set eternity in the heart. Just as the migratory bird sees the vision of its native land, no matter where it is born, so the heart of man naturally reaches out toward eternity. Never has bird, beast or insect been lead astray by their God-given instincts. Do you think that God would plant the holiest of instincts in the human soul and then permit it to utterly mislead that soul in its longing and aspirations after immortality into life beyond? No, never! Thank God there is a reality to satisfy that instinct, that longing. Even as God gives the birds the instinct to fly south and find their winter home, so man knows that the same, all-wise God has given reality to his longing for immortality.

It is said that when a certain soldier lad was asked, "How do you fare?" he replied, "How do things fare with me? I sleep in mud, I bathe in blood, but my soul is in the stars." So with man; he may be dealing with the clay and see the havoc of sin all about him, but his soul is in the stars through faith in Jesus Christ.

Dean Charles Brown of Yale University said, "There are three things that I could never believe: 1) that God would create a world like ours and then turn His back upon it; 2) that He would create man and then desert him at the grave; 3) that He would plant a desire for immortality in the human heart, and fail to make adequate provisions for its realization."

We know there is a future life because of the incompleteness of this life. We live only a fragment of what we seem to need. If death is the common end of all men, then such a terminus to life throws confusion into man's moral ideas, for it shocks him to believe that Elijah, Jezebel, John the Baptist, Herodias, Paul and Nero share at death exactly the same fate—annihilation.

There is nothing to indicate that man's life on earth is one of God's finished chapters. The incompleteness of life is shocking when we think of the great number who never found their place or niche in this world. Principal John Caird of Edinburgh said, "Man's intellectual and moral endowments are on a scale immeasurably larger than the needs of this present life, or that is required for any attainment in knowledge of goodness, which even the noblest and the best men reach in their earthly existence. Therefore, we can only account for the disproportion by the conception of a future life in which these endowments shall find adequate scope and employment."

The best developments of this life are only fragmentary, and the soul needs another life in which to continue its work. The body reaches a peak and begins to deteriorate; but not so with the soul. Man's soul is limitless. Man's soul is fluttering within like a caged bird. He is the noblest creature on earth and at the same time the most miserable. He has greater gifts and higher qualities than any other visible being, and yet he, and only he, is lonely, dejected, sad and sorrowful.

Man alone carries with him a heavy heart. The flocks and herds upon a thousand hills, the myriad forms of insect life, every winged fly and tuneful beetle, the fish that gaily sport and gambol in the rivers and the seas, all confine the end of their being. Not a thought of future want disturbs their perfect tranquility. But never so with man. He only is never satisfied, no matter what his wealth, fame, knowledge, power or earthly pleasures. Man's soul is restless. God made the beast that perishes to find its every desire gratified, while man is created with immortal longings which shall have no satisfactory response, either in time or eternity. Only for the Christian is there the promise of satisfaction. Augustine said, "Thou hast made us for Thyself, O Lord; and our heart is restless until it rests in Thee."

Why does the Christian have a tranquility that the world does not know? Because in this life he becomes the inheritor of eternal life. In that quality of life there is the assurance that he will not only live a life of God-consciousness now, but he will live when the sun is ashes and the stars have gone out forever. "I shall be satisfied, when I awake, with thy likeness" (Psa. 17:15). It is for this purpose God has given us this insatiable thirst. Man pants after happiness infinite in duration. His natural hopes and desires run beyond the bounds of time. His "soul, uneasy and confined from home, rests and expiates in a life to come."

Henry Thomas, the writer of those classic volumes on the history of civilization, had completed only two of an intended six-volume work. His last words were, "My books, my books," for his plans were incomplete.

The great Disraeli said in death, "I am overwhelmed." He was thinking of the incompleteness of his life's work and plans.

The great masterpiece, The Transfiguration, hangs in the Vatican unfinished because the hand of Raphael was stilled in death before the picture was completed. He left but a fragment of the possibilities within his soul.

Victor Hugo said, "I feel in myself the future life. Winter is on my head, but eternal spring is in my heart. The nearer I approach the end, the plainer I hear around me the immortal symphonies of the world that invites me. For a half century I have been writing my thoughts in prose, verse, history, philosophy, drama, romance, tradition, satire, ode, and song. I have tried all, but I feel that I have not said a thousandth part of what is in me. When I go down to the grave I can say, like so many others, I have finished my days' work, but I cannot say I have finished my life's work; my life's work will begin again the next morning. The tomb is not a blind alley, it's a thoroughfare that closes on the twilight to open in the eternal dawn." He had placed his faith in the conqueror of death, Jesus Christ.

Think of the many who died in the prime of usefulness, their lives unfinished, incomplete. David Brainerd, Henry Martyn, Robert Murray McCheyne—great giants in their spiritual effectiveness—scarcely lived to thirty years. Are they not going on in the next life in the service of God? Many of those who did achieve died at the very beginning of their achievement.

Dying at 32, Frederick W. Robertson, exclaimed, "It is all a mystery; man is like a candle blown out by a puff of wind." Keats, the poet, dying at 22, wrote his own epitaph: "Here lies one whose name is written in water." Raphael and Burns died at 38; Mozart at 36; Shelley, the poet at 30. To these we could add an endless list of those who died at the very beginning of a prophetic career. If there is not another world for their dreams and ambitions to come to fruition, then there is something tremendously wrong with this world. If this is all, life here is only a cruel mockery and there is no tragedy like this tragedy anywhere in the universe. There must be another answer —a better explanation.

Dr. Clinton Holt, a young Christian physician and one of the brightest students to attend the University of Southern California, was leading some young YMCA boys on a hike. He was accidentally killed while rescuing a Negro lad from death by a falling boulder. He pushed the terrified youth to safety but the boulder crashed into him with full impact. It is unthinkable that such a life is forever quenched and the flame has gone out, never to be lighted again. Rather we believe that he is sitting at the feet of the Great Physician, scaling heights undreamed of on this earth.

We measure things only from a temporal vantage point and from the past and the present but we must remember that to our Lord there is no past, present or future. It is all one vast present. He knows the end from the beginning and His wisdom is greater than ours.

Think of the five young men who died in the Ecuadorian jungle, twentieth century martyrs for the Christian faith. These five unfinished symphonies—five magnificent lives, were with us in this world for such a short time. Are they not living on in the next life in the visible presence of Jesus Christ? Our highest and best thought causes us to answer an unhesitating "Yes."

A little girl was dying. The doctor, believing her in a coma, said, "Her little life is just ending." She opened her eyes at that precise moment and said, "No doctor, my life is not ending; it is just beginning." She died with the smile of heaven on her face.

This life is only an introduction, a preparation for the life that you are to live in eternity, with God or without God, on the basis of your own personal choice. All life is a school and we are getting ready for the great commencement day and the entrance into the life of marvelous possibilities. This human individual, this conscious personality, this mysterious self shall have fully developed faculties and powers unhampered and unhindered forever. Our present life is only an introduction and preparation for the life to come, a life spent either in the presence of God, or outside the presence of God, forever, and you decide before you make the journey.

The wonderful powers of the human mind and its susceptibility of improvement argue the immortality of the soul. When we stop to think of the intellectual heights men have reached and we see some of the powers of the human mind, there seems to be no limit to intellectual development and improvement. Even in the short space allotted to man on earth, how grand are his achievements. He sweeps the heavens with his telescope and numbers and names the stars. He whitens the seas with ships of commerce and belts the continents with steel. He flies like a bird through the air at a speed surpassing sound. He goes under the water like a fish. In conquest of the space above him, he orbits the earth at 18,000 miles an hour, in a feat requiring mathematical calculations that are astronomical in their exactness and minuteness. He weighs the earth and measures the distance to the most remote planet. He builds towering skyscrapers and plucks messages from ethereal waves. He explores the dark caverns of the earth and ransacks the sepulchre of the ocean. He analyzes the elemental principles of the invisible atmosphere. He splits the mighty atom, harnesses the lightning flash, stores and uses its power.

No wonder a heathen philosopher said, "When I consider the wonderful activity of the mind, so great a memory of the past and such a capacity for what is future, when I behold such a number of arts and sciences and such a multitude of discoveries, I am firmly persuaded that a nature that contains so many things within itself cannot be merely mortal."

Is it not reasonable to infer that minds so admirably constituted and endowed must be designed for something higher than this world affords? As Dr. Clarence True Wilson said, "What an impeachment it would be on the wisdom and goodness of God to suppose that He had created minds with such vast and inconceivable powers only that He might dash them with their frail tabernacle in pieces at death; that He had lighted such intellectual lamps, beaming forth amid the darkness and obstructions of earth with surpassing brilliance and beauty only that He might quench them in the gloomy night of annihilation. The soul's capacity for endless improvement, service, and worship points to a future life, which will make possible greater future development than we achieved here."

Sir Isaac Newton had a mind that could master the most profound truths as easily as an average man can handle the ABC's. One day someone complimented him on his vast learning. He humbly replied, "I seem to be but a child picking up a few pebbles on the shore, while the great ocean of truth stretches on unexplored before me." The mind of man possesses faculties demanding eternal time for development. They are God-given, and God will satisfy them with more than a little handful of earthly time.

Life's inequalities demand a life beyond the boundaries of time. Justice demands another life. In the mind of man, faith in God and faith in right are linked together. "Shall not the Judge of all the earth do right?" (Gen. 18:25) is the granite platform upon which rests the structure of man's hope.

Man is a moral being. This means that he distinguishes between right and wrong and that his conscience within him is the oracle of God. In the government of God, then, virtue must be rewarded and vice must be punished. Things are not right down here. God started them right; but man, the fool he has always been, upset the plan. This world affords no full vindication of justice and right.

The future life is a necessity to vindicate God's moral character. That there is sin and punishment for sin, we daily witness; but there is not a reckoning for *all* sin in this world, to satisfy the claims of righteousness and justice. Do we not see evil go undetected and bad men pass unpunished? Injustice is seen everywhere in human society. Are these wrongs never to be righted? They certainly are not in this life, for they are often continued to its close. Men do not receive their full reward or punishment in this life. Many times the innocent are punished and the guilty go free. Tyrants are enthroned and saints are sent to the dungeon. Vice wears the purple and virtue wears the rags. Nero, Diocletian and the rest of their ilk sat upon the throne, while Paul was beheaded and Huss was burned at the stake.

Things will be balanced in the world to come. If God is just, there must be a heaven and a hell beyond this life. If there is no heaven, what recompense did Paul receive for the stones, the stripes that stung him well nigh to death and for the ax that chopped off his head; or Savonarola for the flames that licked up his blood on the square of San Marco near the palace and the church? Shall the Son of God be crucified and never be exalted?

Justice cries out there is a heaven where those who have lived for God shall dwell with Him. Justice cries out there is a hell for the Christ-rejector who trods underfoot the blood of the covenant whereby we are cleansed. Somewhere there must be an equalization bureau where perfect justice is meted out, and only immortality can supply it.

These are only rational grounds for believing that man lives after death, and helpful as these intimations are, they are not evidences or proofs of immortality. There is a vast difference between these questionings and suggestions of our own hearts and the majestic words of our Lord Jesus Christ, "I am the resurrection and the life: he that believeth in me, though he were dead, yet shall he live: and whosoever liveth and believeth in me shall never die" (John 11:25,26). The heart's intimations of life after death show how natural and reasonable the doctrine is, and when the revelation came through Jesus Christ, when He, by the invasion of our world, brought "immortality to light by the Gospel," it was a revelation that was in harmony with the deepest desires in the heart of man. Deep calleth unto deep.

When Columbus was sailing his frail caravels toward the undiscovered continent of the west, he saw in the sea floating leaves and branches that told him he must be nearing another world. Assured by that conviction, he sailed ever on, until at length the sands of the Bahamas shone white in the moonlight.

Wind and tide carry man across the ocean of existence. He cannot see the place where he is going, nor can he speak to any ships returning from that mysterious land, but in the affections and longing of his heart, in the deepest instincts of his being, in the shadow-like brevity and the pitiful incompleteness of his life, in the longing for justice, he sees portents and intimations, floating messengers of the unseen, on the wastes of time's ocean. These tell him there is the shore of another world.

> *"A land of pure delight,*
> *Where saints immortal reign;*
> *Where infinite day excludes the night*
> *And pleasures banish pain."*

We believe in the future life, not only because of these intimations, but because God says so. The intimations are only the leaves and the branches that float on the surface to tell us that land is ahead. The reason we know it is there is because Jesus Christ is our spiritual Columbus. He has travelled beyond the sunset and the night. He has come through the grave and the gate of death. He says to you and to me: "I am the resurrection . . . because I live, ye shall live also." Without a relationship to Jesus Christ you have no hope for a happy, glorious immortality. You will exist, but you will exist without God, without hope forever and forever.

There are just two worlds ahead. One is a world where men live with Christ, men who have been transformed into the glory of His image by the miracle of the new birth, who are adapted to live in that world because of the transformation that has taken place.

The other world is an empty world, one where men go who do not choose to fulfill their lives in God, where the image of God remains defaced for all the endless aeons of eternity, where men go who did not choose the life that was proffered and offered in the resurrection of Jesus Christ. You decide! You choose! Once the soul is created, it can never be destroyed. It is indestructible. Yes, you will survive death—with God, or without Him.

chapter three

THE FRONTIER
OF THE SUPERNATURAL

"But there is a spirit (in the Hebrew it is the vital force, a spirit of intelligence) in man; and the inspiration of the Almighty giveth them understanding" (Job 32:8).

" . . . the Lord . . . stretcheth forth the heavens, and layeth the foundation of the earth, and formeth the spirit of man within him" (Zech. 12:1).

" . . . and I pray God your whole spirit and soul and body be preserved blameless unto the coming of our Lord Jesus Christ" (I Thess. 5:23).

"For ye are bought with a price: therefore glorify God in your body, and in your spirit, which are God's" (I Cor. 6:20).

"For what man knoweth the things of a man, save the spirit of man which is in him? . . . " (I Cor. 2:11).

We have concluded that man is more than body, brain, and breath; that there is an inner man inside the outer man and this inner man survives the destruction of the outer man. When this body (the outer man) sleeps in the grave, the real man (the inner man), the soul, will not go to sleep with the body. It will leave the body and go to some other sphere, higher or lower, above or below. The body is but the tabernacle in which the soul dwells. Some day the soul will move out of the house it has inhabited for a time; but that body will be renovated, repaired, renewed, glorified, and reunited with the soul. This is the clear testimony of I Corinthians 15.

French scientist Professor Charles Henry declared that the human soul, that mysterious thing that is not a "thing," that was accepted only through faith, can now be measured. For the first time, science admits tangible proof of the soul's existence. Says the scientist: "Religion is right. We never completely die. There is a certain electrical radiation, or biological vibration, that goes on and on. Set free by death, it seeks another envelope or body, because only by so doing can it establish this equilibrium." This is in perfect correspondence and harmony with the findings of Dr. Gustav Stromberg, as revealed in his book, *The Soul of the Universe,* and the conclusions of Dr. H. S. Burr of the neuro-anatomy division of Yale University.

Francis Miller suggests that the thinker and the brain are two separate entities — that the brain, like the hand, is only the instrument of the thinker. Mr. Miller asked these questions: "Did surgical science ever find a thought in the brain of a human being? Did it ever locate an idea in the brain of man? Did it ever find a railroad engine? A jet liner? Or a battleship? A radio or a television set? A rocket with its orbiting capsule? A Manhattan skyscraper? The Holland Tunnel? The Golden Gate Bridge? Has any of these ever been found in the head of a man? All of these emanated from and grew out of an idea, an intangible, undiscovered thought in the mind of a man."

Destroy man's achievements so that not one exists, but retain the ideas that correspond to these accomplishments, and they could all be brought into existence again. Every mechanism, every structure that man has built is but the materialization of one of those unmeasurable, invisible ideas. Yet no surgeon has ever been able to dissect or perform an operation on an idea, or remove one from the human brain. What scientist ever saw thought? Yet who would deny that thought is the most powerful force in the world? Did anyone ever find love or hate in the heart of a man or see it anywhere in his anatomy? Did anyone ever locate courage, fear, joy, sorrow, good or bad in the organism of man? To reflect upon such questions makes it clear once again that man lives in a physical body, but man *himself* is soul and spirit.

One of the strongest proofs of the existence of God is that man has in his mind the idea of God. How, if there is no God, could we conceive of God? A. Cressy Morrison, author of the book, *Man Does Not Stand Alone,* and former president of the New York Academy of Science, says:

> The conception of God arises from a divine faculty of man unshared by the rest of our world, the faculty we call imagination. By its power man, and man alone, can find the evidence of things unseen. The vista that power opens up is unbounded. Indeed, as man's perfected imagination becomes a spiritual reality, he may discern in all the evidences of design and purpose the great truth that heaven is wherever and whatever, that God is everywhere, and in everything, but nowhere so close as in our hearts. It is scientifically, as well as imaginatively true that, as the Psalmist said, "The heavens declare the glory of God, and the firmament showeth His handiwork."

Dr. Harry Rimmer told the story of a famous American novelist who prided himself upon his skepticism. Speaking at a public gathering in Kansas City, he made a sweeping denial of the existence of anything supernatural, including the existence of God. Laying his watch upon the table in front of him, he startled his credulous audience with a magnificent dare. In words that rang out over the awed hush of his listening audience, he said, "There is no God anywhere. If there is a God, I defy Him. I will give God Almighty fifteen minutes to come down here and strike me dead, and if He doesn't do it, I will have proved that He does not exist!"

With bated breath the audience waited until the fifteen minutes had passed. Solemnly pocketing his watch, the lecturer triumphantly announced, "I have proved there is no God," and took his seat amid the applause of the so-called intelligentsia.

The national press seized upon this sensational demonstration with a flood of editorial comments. The best remarks, in the opinion of Dr. Rimmer, were those of Arthur Brisbane. The opinions of the brilliant Mr. Brisbane were read perhaps by more people than any other column published in America. Mr. Brisbane began by referring to the novelist's dare and the failure of God to answer. Then, without any personal remarks on the subject, he wrote:

> Out in the desert of New Mexico a colony of little red ants decided to move from their old home to a new one. As they were hurrying busily across the plain, their progress was suddenly interrupted by two bright, shiny streaks of steel that intersected their pathway. An inquiring ant said to his neighbor, "What is this barrier across our path?"
>
> This wise and intelligent neighbor said, "It is the right-of-

way of the Santa Fe Railway."

The first ant said, "What is a railway, and what is the Santa Fe?"

In response to this question, the intelligent ant gave a graphic description of the mighty railway system called the Santa Fe and told how it spanned two-thirds of the continent with this girding roadbed of steel. He told of the mighty steel horses, snorting smoke and fire, that drew a race of super beings, called humans, at an incredible speed across the desert. When he had finished his description of this mighty transportation system, the skeptical ant said, "I do not believe a word of it. How would it keep on running?"

So, the intelligent ant described the personnel who operate this great system, and told how a man named Benjamin Storey lived in a place called Chicago and guided the destinies of this vast concern. The skeptical ant drew himself up on his hind legs and stared at the gleaming wall of steel. In stentorian tones he announced, "I deny there is a Santa Fe Railway and that it has a president. If there is such a man as Benjamin Storey, I will give him fifteen minutes to come out from Chicago and step on me to prove his existence!"

Mr. Brisbane humorously concluded by saying, "Can't you imagine the busy president of the Santa Fe Railway, with the destinies of that great concern in his hands, closing his desk and suspending his business to dash out to New Mexico to step on one red ant, just to prove that he did exist?"

Said Dr. Rimmer, "This ingenious and clever retort so laughed the famous skeptic out of court that we have heard nothing of his demonstration since." The parable is exact. Men who deny the existence of God are, by comparison, in the identical class with insects that deny the existence of men.

Just as one of the proofs of God's existence is the fact that man can conceive of Him, so the same argument holds good when we come to the doctrine of immortality. In spite of the evidence of death all about him, in spite of the certain death that awaits him personally, man has a conception of immortality. If man were a creature destined to nothingness in the grave, how could he have the impression of life after death? The very fact that men in all ages have had this instinct is, in itself, of tremendous significance.

The plan of the Creator in this world is to supply a suitable organ wherever He implants the instinct or capacity. The bee has the instinct to secrete honey, and honey and wax are provided. The bird has the instinct to fly and the wing with which to fly. The fish has the instinct to swim and the fins with which to swim. The ear is made for hearing and the eye for seeing. Are we to think that this great plan of God breaks down only when we come to the highest creature and the highest instinct of that creature, which is life after death?

How deep, universal, and ancient that instinct for immortality is may be seen from all those processes in nature that are similar to life emerging out of death. This is often spoken of as an argument from analogy. An Egyptian saw the beetle crawl from its filthy bed of dung and in his temples hung up the golden scarabaeus as the symbol of life to come. He saw the butterfly escape in radiant glory from her seeming deadness and on his tomb carved a butterfly as the symbol of the resurrection. When the ice and snow began to melt and the south winds began to blow softly, when spring blew her clarion over the dreaming earth, man saw the dead branches bud and put forth new leaves. In the luxuriant burst of springtime he saw the sure token of a new and deathless life.

In a hundred different forms man has desired to repeat

the myth of the Phoenix, that fabled bird, which, after subsisting for 500 years, loaded its wings with spices, flew into the temple, and burned to ashes upon the altar. Out of the ashes the new bird emerged, saluted the priest, and flew away. Therefore, man in his unenlightened condition, placed the Phoenix in his temples as the symbol of life everlasting.

These analogies, of course, prove nothing. The beetle, the butterfly and the tree only *seem* to be dead. Yet the appeal to man of these processes in nature show how deep, even in pagan darkness, was his instinct for immortality. Animals are not troubled with the hopes that fill the heart of man. The spot on which they tread yields them all the happiness of which they are capable. A little grass satisfies the sheep, a little blood gluts the tiger. The only creature that looks beyond himself and is not all in all to himself is man. The preacher of Ecclesiastes is thought to have struck this note when he said: "He has made everything beautiful in its time; He also has planted eternity in men's heart and mind [a divinely implanted sense of a purpose working through the ages which nothing under the sun, but only God, can satisfy], yet so that man cannot find out what God has done from the beginning to the end" (Eccles. 3:11 Amplified O.T.).

The truth of immortality is one of the most practical truths in the world. Believe in it and you live like it. Noble thoughts are matched by a noble life. Fail to believe in it, think of it as only a dim possibility, or discard it altogether, and immediately your moral and spiritual life is weakened. Renan, the agnostic, said that one evidence for the truth of immortality may be found in the nobility of behavior it inspires.

If death ends all, what an imposter is the system of laws on which our society is founded. If we must wholly perish, the maxims of charity and justice and the precepts of honor and friendship are but empty words. Why should they be binding if only in this life we have hope? What duty do we owe to the dead, to the living or to ourselves, if all will be nothing? If restitution terminates with the grave, morality is a bugbear of human invention. What do the sweet ties of kindred matter if we shall not live again? What sanctity is there to the last wish of the dying, if death is a wall instead of a door? What is obedience to laws but a senseless servitude? What is justice but an unwarrantable infringement upon liberty? What are the laws of marriage but a vain scruple? And what is government but an imposition on credulity if death ends all?

One nation tried to destroy belief in God and immortality. France, at the outset of the French Revolution, decreed in national convention there was no God and death was an eternal sleep. Sunday, the Christian's day of worship, was abolished. The Bible was dragged along the streets in the spirit of derision and contempt, infidelity reigned and frightful was its reign. Its crown was terror, its throne the guillotine, its sceptre the battle ax, its palace yard a field of blood and its royal robes dripped with human gore. Gutters were filled with the torn shreds of human flesh. Property was confiscated. The morning breeze and evening wind bore across the vine-clad hills of France the cries of suffering and shrieks of terror. To save the metropolis and the kingdom from utter desolation, the infidel authorities had to reinstate the observance of Sunday as a day of public worship.

In our time there is another system trying the same godlessness, and it will inevitably destroy itself. Its horrible destiny is already written. When belief in God and immortality die out in the human heart, the flood gates of vice open wide, plunge the world into the grave of despair, and consign humanity to the hopelessness of a meaningless existence.

Belief in the future life inspires a man to climb; not to believe, forces him to deteriorate. It is true that without this vision men perish. We rise to alpine heights in the glory of manhood when we believe in our eternal life. It is this truth that furnishes us with courage and cheerfulness in meeting life's trials and carrying life's burdens. It gives us a holy ambition for the making of life and the rendering of service. It is a great life that is lived constantly in the conscious light of eternity.

"The heart hath reason of its own," said Pascal, "of which the mind knows nothing." No survey of the intimations of immortality would be complete without paying tribute to this reason of the heart. Sometimes we learn more from the heart than we do from rationalization. Everyone who has loved and lost knows what this reason is.

The Gospels tell us that after the disciples had inspected the empty sepulchre, they went away again to their own homes; "but Mary stood without the sepulchre weeping." And there, through all the ages since death first came into the world, Mary, symbol of grief, stands weeping and refusing to be comforted. So love weeps for friends separated from it by death and finds no real ray of comfort, save the hope of meeting again on some far-away shore. It may be that "it is better to have loved and lost than never to have loved at all," but that "better" is far from best.

Recollection spends its hours in sweet counsel with those it loved who are now gone, but memory cannot fill the aching void. Indeed, our memories emphasize the change that has taken place and send the mourning heart away empty. There is but one thought that comforts the heart and that is the thought of seeing again, in the glorious morning of another life, those faces we have loved long since and lost awhile.

If we do not meet again and know one another in heaven, our love for our dead ought to die when they are laid in the grave; but we do not cease to love them. Neither do we love them less but rather more than we love the living, with a love more unselfish and with less taint of earthliness. If we, with our limitations, can love so ardently, how much more those with ever-broadened faculties, having entered into the fulness of life, can love with a deeper passion and a more enduring intensity. The yearning for eternal life for those we love involves the certainty that the great heart of God will give to us this lofty desire. Our Lord said, " . . . I go to prepare a place for you . . . " (John 14:2,3).

I have a date with my wonderful Dad. Among other things he said to me on his last night in this world was, "Son, I'll see you in the morning."

There is definite evidence of the existence of a supernatural world. No sphere of investigation by man's inquiring mind can thrust him on mental expeditions so susceptible to deceit and fraud as the field of the supernatural. When we refer to evidences from a supernatural source, we simply mean those facts and objective experiences which have unquestionable impact upon the consciousness of the race. Professor Otto mentions what he calls our experience of the "Numinous." Those who have not met this term may be introduced to it in the writings of C. S. Lewis, by the following illustration:

> Suppose you were told that there was a tiger in the next room. You would know that you were in danger and would probably feel fear. But if you were told there was a ghost in the next room and believed it, you would feel indeed what is often called fear, but a different kind. It would not be based on the knowledge of danger, for no one is primarily afraid of what a ghost may do to him, but of the mere fact that it is a ghost. It is "uncanny" rather than dangerous, and that special kind of fear it excites may be called dread. With the "uncanny" one has reached the fringes of the Numinous.

> Now suppose that you were told simply that there was a mighty spirit in the next room and you believed it. Your feelings would be even less like the mere fear of danger but the disturbance would be profound. You would feel wonder, a certain shrinking, a sense of inadequacy to cope with such a visitant, prostrate before it, an emotion that might be expressed in Shakespeare's words, "under it my genius is rebuked." This feeling may be described as awe, and the object which excited it as the "Numinous." We do not know how far back in human history this feeling goes but it is probably as old as humanity itself. It does not disappear from the mind of man with the growth of knowledge and civilization.

> This awe is not the result of an inference from the visible universe; it is the result of an inference from the invisible universe. It is undoubtedly the direct experience of the really supernatural. When a man passes from physical fear to dread and awe, he makes a sheer jump and apprehends something which could never be given, as danger is, by the physical facts and the logical deductions from them.

Mental telepathy, premonition, and the Numinous all infer there is a supernatural world. Also the philosophy which men call "the fourth dimension" was evolved to give a demonstration of the reality of this sphere that is superior to nature. C. S. Lewis further develops this idea when he says that if we could conceive of a line that had no breadth or depth, we would have then a first dimension. If this one-dimensional object were a living creature, in the very nature of its form it would know nothing but length. Then, if our imagination can go far enough to conceive of another object that had length and breadth but no depth, which object was endowed with life, we would then have a two-dimensional creature. To this supposition we add a third creature that has length, breadth and height; this would be a third-dimensional being. The second-dimensional creature would gaze upon the one with only one dimension and say, "You look odd to me because there is no breadth to you."

The lower form, knowing only length, would reply, "Breadth? what do you mean by breadth?"

When the creature of the two dimensions tried to expound the philosophy of wideness to the creature who knew only length, this one-dimensional object would probably repudiate the possibility of a dimension of which it knew nothing. We cannot know by nature that which is superior to us. At the same time the creature of three dimensions, looking down from its superior vantage point of height upon the two-dimensional creature, would have difficulty in making this latter form realize that there was a creature of three dimensions. This long and wide object, knowing nothing of height, being unable to look up, would scornfully repudiate the existence of a third sphere.

When we complete the argument, man is a creature of three dimensions. He lives in a space, time, matter world. High above him there is a fourth dimension, which is the spiritual world. Having had no personal and physical experience with that super world, he is incapable of looking into this fourth dimension, which is the world of immortal life. To the experience of man, all life is limited, finite, brief, and certain to conclude. Everything in man's experience has a beginning and an ending. It is impossible to conceive of endless space. Therefore, any fourth-dimensional creatures, not bound by the physical laws of the nature of this planet, who desired to be known to us lesser humans, would have to evolve some form of revelation to make themselves visible to us. This is the logic of the incarnation: "The Word became flesh and dwelt among us."

In the Word of God we find that the fourth-dimension or the spiritual has found a method of revealing itself to us lower creatures. The angels who made an appearance to bring a message from that world to this one clothed themselves in such visible form as may be grasped by human vision. When the cosmic God, who fills the infinitude of endless space, wanted to reveal Himself to us, the only possible way was through the miracle of the incarnation. You can see that the enhumanation of God in the virgin birth of Jesus Christ was the only possible way that God could come out of that fourth dimension and reveal Himself in terms that we could understand. The final and fullest revelation God made of Himself was when He gave us in Christ the effulgence of the Father's glory, the express image of His person (Heb. 1:3).

Einstein said that there is a vast cosmic Intelligence but that this Intelligence is so far beyond the mind of men that man could never even conceive of Him. He said, "I wish he could, but of course he can't."

What does the Word of God say? "The Word (the logos, interpreted by the Greeks as the mind of God) was made flesh, and dwelt among us, (and we beheld his glory, the glory as of the only begotten of the Father,) full of grace and truth" (John 1:14). There is only one way that God could invade the stream of human life and reveal Himself and that was to come out of the fourth dimension into our world by the miracle of parthenogenesis — His virgin birth. He had to be the earthly son of a Heavenly Father and the Heavenly Son of an earthly mother.

On the authority of the Scripture and its historical evidence, we are bold to state there is a sphere of the supernatural. The world of the supernatural is not only complex but is also marvelously complicated. As it is revealed to us in the sacred Word of God, we find that it is highly organized and has a system of governments superior to that which we see among men on this earth. This mystic world contains various orders of beings, even as does the biological world. In that super state there are systems of government and degrees of existence in personality. We must, of course, begin with Almighty God, the Triune, Inter-Personal Being. He is the highest being in the world of the supernatural, whom all others reverence, worship and adore. He is the author and creator of all things, whether they be natural or supernatural.

Apart from the Scripture's divine revelation, there is evidence of psychic phenomena that can only be explained by the existence of the supernatural world. One of the types of psychic evidence would be the purported communication of the living with the spirits of the departed dead. The second type of supernatural evidence would consist of spirit "photographs," manifestations, such as table tilting and rapping and the moving of various physical objects, as are common in spiritist's séances. This so-called psychic evidence reveals to us a world that fills us with terror. A world explained by the Word of God, a world inhabited by superhuman creatures called demons.

The subject of the life beyond and what happens after death should be of intense interest to you. When that last hour comes, when earth recedes and heaven opens, when the voices of earth are no longer heard and the faces we have seen and loved have faded from our view, when earth's night is at hand and we are laid away for our last sleep, when we come to the end of our journey here on earth and take the road that leads to eternity, God grant that it may be well with us, that we may hear the voice of the Son of God bidding us welcome. May there be friends to meet us on that other shore. May our eventide be light and our path be as the path of the righteous, which shineth brighter and brighter unto the perfect day. May we be "carried by the angels" into Jesus' presence and rest in the arms of God. "And this is the record, that God hath given to us eternal life, and this life is in his Son. He that hath the Son hath life; and he that hath not the Son of God hath not life" (I John 5:11-12). He is the only one who has stepped out of the fourth dimension, and He is the only one who can take *us* into that fourth-dimension life. Here is the true answer to immortality: "And this is life eternal, that they might know thee the only true God, and Jesus Christ, whom thou hast sent" (John 17:3).

During the heartless tyranny of the Middle Ages, it seems as though the princes and kings vied with each other to see who could resort to the most terrible and cruel methods of torture. One method, used by the Hohenstaufen House in Germany, was to put their victims into what appeared to be a comfortable room. The prisoner might think this a punishment not to be despised but the vindicative persecutors knew better. In a few days the victim discovered that the room had contracted. The walls were gradually coming together and all at once his horrible fate flashed upon his mind. In oiled and silent grooves, the metal walls were drawing closer and closer. Finally he could no longer lie down. Next he had room only to stand erect. Frantically he put his hands against the iron walls to hold them, but silently, relentlessly, they closed upon him and crushed him to death.

What a picture this is of the man who has no hope in Christ, no hope for the world to come. The years such a man lives are the walls of his prison and every day they are contracting about him. Things may seem pleasant for a time, but with every pulse beat the iron walls draw closer and closer about his soul. Every hour that passes is one chance less to gain eternal life, to gain glory and honor and immortality. The only hope of escape is through Jesus Christ. Every voice of mercy, every striving of the Holy Spirit is an angel of God knocking at the door of your narrowing prison, to tell you of the refuge that you can find in Jesus Christ. "I am come that they might have life and that they might have it more abundantly" (John 10:10). "I am the resurrection, and the life; he that believeth in me, though he were dead, yet shall he live" (John 11:25). "For God so loved the world, that he gave his only begotten Son, that whosoever believeth in him should not perish, but have everlasting life" (John 3:16).

Bishop Berggrav, when asked what death means to a believer, replied, "A farmer was taking his little boy to a distant place. As they were walking along they came to a rickety old bridge over a turbulent stream. It could not be forded, so the bridge had to be used. The little boy became quite apprehensive. 'Father, do you think it is safe to cross the stream?'

"The father answered, 'Son, I'll hold your hand. You put your hand in mine.' So the little boy put his hand in his father's. With trepidation he walked by his father's side across the bridge. They finally made their way to their destination. That was in the daylight. Eventide wore on.

"The night shadows were falling by the time they were returning home. As the little fellow walked by his father's side, he said, 'Father, what about that stream? What about that rickety old bridge? I'm frightened. Oh, my father, you just don't know how frightened I am.'

"The big, powerful farmer reached down, took the little fellow in his arms and said, 'Now you just stay in my

49

arms. You'll feel safe.' As the farmer walked down the road with his precious burden, the little boy fell sound asleep.

"The next morning he woke up, safe at home in bed. The sun was streaming through the window. He never even knew that he had been taken safely across the bridge and over the turbulent waters.

"That is the death of a Christian."

"I will fear no evil for thou art with me." The Christian falls asleep in Jesus and wakes up in the glory of His presence.

I agree with the editorial writer who said, "I don't want to go alone. I want to go all the way with Jesus Christ." How are *you* going?

chapter four

THE SPHERE OF
THE SUPERNATURAL

"In conclusion be strong — not in yourselves but in the Lord, in the power of his boundless resource. Put on God's complete armour, so that you can successfully resist all the devil's methods of attack. For our fight is not against any physical enemy: it is against organizations and powers that are spiritual. We are up against the unseen power that controls this dark world, and spiritual agents from the very headquarters of evil. Therefore you must wear the whole armour of God that you may be able to resist evil in its day of power, and that even when you have fought to a standstill you may still stand your ground" (Eph. 6:10-13, Phillips).

In asking the question: "Does any part of the human being survive the death of the physical body?" the Word of God has the final answer. However, extensive research in Extra Sensory Perception has indicated, in its freedom from the effects of time and space, the possibility of survival beyond death.

In citing evidence for the supernatural world we have mentioned what Professor Otto calls the experience of the Numinous — a dread or awe experienced by man that is not the result of any inference from the visible universe. It is undoubtedly the direct experience of the really supernatural. As C. S. Lewis says, when a man passes from physical fear to dread and awe, he makes a sheer jump and apprehends something which could never be given (as danger is) by physical facts and logical deductions from these facts. Thus the Numinous indicates there is a supernatural world.

We have also discussed the possibility of what men of philosophy call "the fourth dimension." This was evolved to give a demonstration of the reality of this sphere that is superior to nature. Man is a creature of three dimensions. He lives in the very confining limitations of a space, time, material universe. High above him, or all about him — perhaps closer to him than he realizes — there is a fourth dimension which is the non-physical, supernatural or spiritual world. He is unable to relate himself physically to this fourth-dimensional world of spiritual life.

The science of parapsychology is giving us evidence of a world that is non-physical. The word "para" means beyond. The parapsychologists rally behind the knowledge that this force, which is outside the natural world and of which they have already proved the reality, will in time revolutionize our concept of the universe to an extent beyond the wildest imagination. There is no telling how far the parapsychology research will lead us. The proof that there is something extra-physical or spiritual in human personality has momentous implications.

In hypnosis there is observable phenomena that is intriguing. Occasionally dramatic results have occurred in relieving the symptoms of diseases through hypnotic suggestion and in relieving pain; for example, in dentistry and obstetrics. Even the nervous system responds to suggestion. Hypnosis is the inducing of artificial sleep in which the subject is amenable to the suggestions of another. There are varying depths of trance, and suggestions are always within the realm of basic inhibited limitations. A person can be told to jump out a window, but he will refuse. He can be commanded to remove his clothes, but if he is modest he will merely be embarrassed and never comply. Hypnosis seems to remove the inability to recall and allows an exploration of the subconscious mind.

The widely-known mentalist, Dunninger, has demonstrated mental telepathy beyond question, though he would not purport on any occasion to tell anyone's future. There is a vast difference in foretelling the future and merely being able to receive thought impressions that someone by concentration is attempting to send. Research in the field of parapsychology reveals there is not much success in the exchange of thoughts unless both parties agree to cooperate.

Many who claim the ability to "see" an event yet future, merely have ESP, a term meaning, "beyond the power of our natural senses." For instance, Dr. C. Eaton experimented with a medium. He would open a book to a certain page, look at the number of the page, ask the medium at what page the book was open. Immediately the medium would identify the very page. Then he tried it this way. He opened the book without looking at it and after he has asked what page it was and the reply was given, he would look at the page to see the number. Every time this method was used in the experiment, the medium was wrong. Obviously, this was a case of mental telepathy. However, there have been cases in which objects, scenes and experiences have been recognized without another mind engaged in the experiment.

An intriguing study was made at Duke University under the direction of Dr. J. B. Rhine, a professor of parapsychology, in all the areas of ESP. This eminent man has written a book entitled *The Reach of the Mind,* in which he has amassed evidence to support the fact that there are those who are endowed with astounding ability beyond the power of the natural senses.

One little girl was found whose skill was amazing. Using a series of cards bearing five easily distinguishable symbols — a cross, a circle, a square, a star, and three parallel wavy lines, twenty-five in all — this little girl could make a perfect score at any time. Never seeing the cards and allowing someone else to look at them, she could write down the symbol of each card chosen. Distance had no effect upon her powers.

From North Carolina to Yugoslavia, one series of controlled experiments was actually conducted between Dr. Marchesi of Zagred, Yugoslavia, and collaborators at Duke University in Durham, North Carolina, with dramatic results. Exhaustive research has handed down the verdict that distance has no effect whatsoever upon ESP. Since physical energy is affected by distance, it would seem to indicate that ESP must be non-physical.

Cases of clairvoyance have been demonstrated in which objects, scenes, and experiences have been recognized without another mind engaged in the experiment. In some experiments cards were placed face down and the subject would identify the cards with an accuracy beyond mathematical probability. This demonstrates the existence of mental telepathy for which there is no physical explanation.

Emanuel Swedenborg, the Swedish scientist and philosopher, while in Goteborg in 1759, described a fire blazing in Stockholm three hundred miles away. He gave a detailed account of the fire to city authorities, even naming the owner of the burned house. He further stated the time when the fire was under control and put out. The accuracy of his clairvoyant vision was confirmed several days later by royal messengers. There are multiplied thousands of similar documented evidences of clairvoyancy.

A study is now in progress concerning premonition. There is an indication from the scientific data gathered that we have the explanation for that strange way in which many people have known of the death of a loved one before they are told about it, even knowing the exact hour. It would seem that the dying person sends that fact *via* final mental or spiritual exertion, and an impression is relayed.

Arthur Godfrey, the well-known radio and T. V. personality, tells an interesting story of how, while at sea in the Navy, he suddenly knew of his father's death and all the circumstances that were incident to it. He even identified the clothing his father was wearing at the time.

Much of the success of fortune tellers is the ability to receive impressions from the minds of their clients rather than their clairvoyant powers. The Psychical Research Society believes that only two per cent of the fortune tellers are able to predict the future with any dependable accuracy. This subject will be discussed later. But it must be said, this is an extremely dangerous experimentation, because it is not a contact with God, but rather a contact with the sinister, evil world controlled by Satan himself. One incontrovertible conclusion comes out of this study: man is infinitely more than a biological mechanism, a mere protoplastic mass that is waiting to become manure. There is a sphere about us to which we are just being introduced, a sphere that knows none of the limitations of our three-dimensional world.

The Word of God tells us that this supernatural sphere is composed of two complex worlds: a righteous spiritual world inhabited by benevolent, good beings; and an evil spiritual world inhabited by malicious beings. These two worlds are locked in a conflict that will be resolved in the final triumph of the righteous.

All of this adds up to demonstrate the existence of a fourth-dimensional world in which time, space, and matter are non-existent. We are prone to speak of this spiritual world as being far-distant and separated from us by eons of time and space; but evidence would indicate that the world of the natural and the supernatural are not far apart.

Nothing but the veil of the flesh separates the present from the future, the natural from the supernatural. Sometimes that veil wears thin and we are accorded a glimpse, a vision of the spiritual, while still in the body. We might even say that the barrier that separates us from the eternal world is not so much a wall as a curtain. Men of flesh and blood cannot enter the spiritual world, but we do indeed live upon its very border. As close as is the breath of death, so close are we to the borderland of the world of the supernatural.

The existence of that world is also an indication of the probability of immortality. It must be admitted that sometimes the dying seem to pause momentarily with one foot in each world, looking both ways. Many authentic records have been given us of so-called deathbed visions. Many times it seems that spiritual vision and discernment are greatly intensified and heightened as death approaches. Sometimes what is seen is described to those who may be near. This is not as true now as it was in the days before men died under the influence of strong drugs and sedation.

Dr. Harry Rimmer recalls an illustration of a young woman named Dorothy who was dying in a California hospital. She had wasted away over a long period of weeks with an incurable disease. In the room with Dorothy were her mother and aunt, who kept a constant vigil by her bedside. One day, as the nurse was quietly giving comfort and attention, the dying young woman, who seemed to be in a state of coma, suddenly shook her head with vigor and said, "No!" Again she shook her head and said, "No!" Then, to the surprise of all, in her weakened condition, she raised herself in bed and looked toward the corner of the room. The other occupants looked in the direction of the glance of the sick one, and to their surprise the wall of the room seemed to have melted away. In place of the hospital walls they clearly saw a garden. Coming down the path of this garden, with a smile on her face and her hands extended in greeting, they saw the form of the grandmother who had gone to be with the Lord more than a year before. They heard the dying girl laugh, and glancing at her saw a smile of delight upon her face. She nodded her head and said, "Oh, if that's the way it is, all right."

Dorothy lay back on the pillow and as a smile of happiness lighted her countenance, the spirit fled her body. The nurse and the other two women hastened to her side. When they thought to look back at the corner of the room where the vision had been, nothing was there but the plain walls of the hospital room.

D. L. Moody at his death said, "God is calling; earth is receding. Heaven is opening before me."

While such evidence is only suggestive, it is at least light through the screen. Such glimpses over the border of the world that now is into the one that shall be may be advanced as at least an indication of immortality.

But now we turn to the most powerful evidence of all. I would rather have the evidence now to be presented than the opinion of all the philosophical literati, scientific dignitaries, and the authorities in every area and realm pertaining to this subject. There is no source of history in the possession of man that is as credible and reliable as is the Book called the Bible. In this Book we rejoice to find that the fourth-dimensional or spiritual world is not only existent but that it has found a method of revealing itself to us lower creatures. What intuition infers and reason demands, the Bible declares.

On the authority of the Scripture and its historical evidence, we are bold to state that there is a sphere of the supernatural. This world is not only complex but marvelously complicated. The angels who made their appearance to bring a message from that world to this one, clothed themselves in such visible form as may be grasped by human vision. According to the Word of God the celestial world is highly organized and has a system of government superior to that which we see among men. This mystic world contains various orders of beings even as does the biological world. In that super state there are degrees of existence and personality beyond anything that we can know. The highest, of course, whom all the others worship and adore, is Almighty God, the Triune Being, the Author and Creator of all things, whether they be natural or supernatural.

In our consideration of this subject it is necessary to consider the broader sphere of the whole universe and not to restrict ourselves to the limited boundaries of the earth. Modern astronomy has presented evidence of the vastness of material creation. Solar systems greater than this extend on beyond the range of human power to comprehend. Other suns, with all that surround them, removed from this earth and its sun by thirty to sixty billion miles, are known to exist.

Camille Flammarion, the celebrated French astronomer, states:

> Then I understood that all the stars which have ever been observed in the sky, the millions of luminous points which constitute the Milky Way, the enumerable celestial bodies, suns of every magnitude and of every degree of brightness, solar systems, planets, satellites, which by millions and hundreds of millions succeed each other in the void around us; that whatever human tongues have designed by the name of universe, do not, in the infinite, represent more than an

archipelago of celestial islands, and not more than a city in a grand total of populations, a town of greater or lesser importance. In this city of the limitless empire, in this town of a land without frontiers, our sun and its system represent a single point, a single house among millions of other habitations. Is our solar system a palace or a hovel in this great city? Probably a hovel. And the earth? The earth is a room in the solar mansion, a small dwelling—miserably small.

We are confronted with the endlessness of space and the fact that our little planet called earth is like a grain of sand in the universe compared with the endlessness of the expanses of galaxies known and unknown that reach out in every direction.

From earliest times men have considered the question: "Is this earth the only inhabited planet?" Science ventures guesses, and our exploration in outer space argues that there is absolutely no evidence of life similar to ours on any of the planets in our solar system. Life as we know it could not exist on any of them. But the Holy Book does disclose that angels dwell in the heavenly spheres in number beyond human computation. They are in subjection to the Lord Jesus Christ (I Peter 3:22). He created this vast, endless universe and all it contains, both visible and invisible (Col. 1:16). No intimation is ever given that these supernatural messengers are limited to the sphere of this earth or restricted to any particular area of the universe. Our Lord said, "In my Father's house are many mansions" (John 14:2). In the Greek it is "many dwelling places." The "Father's house" is no less than the universe in which there are many abodes. Jude asserts that angels have their own dwelling places.

We are told of a class of beings called archangels. Three of these are named in Scripture. Lucifer will be spoken of in detail later. The other two, Gabriel and Michael, are stated to be the messengers of God to man. Michael, we are told in Daniel 12:1, is the head of the armies of heaven. In the Old Testament both these mighty beings enter into God's ministry of prophetic revelation as they come to the aid and comfort of Daniel. In the New Testament, Gabriel is the instrument of the revelation to Mary and Joseph of the supernatural birth of the Lord Jesus Christ. These archangels might be called the rulers or the governors under God of the spiritual world, and under them we are shown a host of living beings called angels. They are mentioned in the Bible a total of 273 times. So great is our reverence for God's Word, and so marvelously have we seen it vindicated in every claim that we cannot believe that the Holy Book would descend to lying 273 times on this subject. We view with confidence the statements of Scripture on this as on all subjects.

In Genesis 16 there is the historical statement of the visit of an angel to Hagar in the time of her trouble. In Genesis 19 two heavenly visitants appeared in Sodom to warn just and righteous Lot of the impending doom of that city. In Genesis 22 a heavenly creature appeared to Abraham when the patriarch was about to offer his son Isaac upon the altar. There is also the record of Jacob's ladder, the host that Jacob saw at Mahanaim, and countless other instances in the first book of the Bible. All these calmly assert, on the authority of the inspiration of the Holy Spirit, the fact of angels as existent beings.

In the book of Exodus it was an angel who called Moses to the presence of God in the burning bush. In the book of Numbers, their presence is frequently seen, as when Balaam's ass was turned aside from the highway by the appearance of a supernatural being. In this brief summary, we have only space to add that in the books of Judges, First and Second Samuel, Kings and Chronicles, Job, Psalms, Ecclesiastes, Isaiah, Daniel, Hosea and Zechariah, the existence of angels is affirmed 112 times.

Angels are set forth as created beings whom we might reverently call God's laborers. They exist to do His will and to perform such service for Him as the works of a spiritual kingdom might call for. That angels are real, living beings, is evidenced by the fact that the Epistle to the Hebrews, in its first two chapters, sets forth seven reasons why Jesus is greater and better than the angels. Very clearly then, angels are as real in personality and existence as was the Lord Jesus Christ when He walked the earth in a physical, bodily form.

We are told again in the Epistle to the Hebrews that man for a little while has been created on a lower plane than the angels. To angels, however, has been given the ministry of protection and defense of needy humans. Whose heart is not thrilled to the happy comfort of Psalm 91:11, 12? Here God's Spirit has promised: "For he shall give His angels charge over thee, to keep thee in all thy ways. They shall bear thee up in their hands, lest thou dash thy foot against a stone." Many saints of the living God have been comforted by this blessed Psalm and even more so by the experience of care and help that comes from this invisible source.

Jesus said, "Take heed that ye despise not one of these little ones; for I say unto you, That in heaven their angels do always behold the face of my Father which is in heaven" (Matt. 18:10). There can be no other inter-pretation here than that Jesus believed in the actual existence of angels. Our Lord, in His infancy, was defended by their ministry, to which He later referred. "And when they were departed, behold, the angel of the Lord appeared to Joseph in a dream, saying, Arise, and take the young child and His mother, and flee into Egypt, and be thou there until I bring thee word: for Herod will seek the young child to destroy Him" (Matt. 2:13). Later on, a celestial visitant said; "Arise, and take the young child and His mother, and go into the land of Israel: for they are dead which sought the young child's life" (Matt. 2:20).

Not only children but all regenerated believers in the Lord Jesus Christ are the beneficiaries of this blessed ministry. Dr. R. A. Torrey believed that whenever a saint dies a convoy of angels ushers that saint into the presence of Jesus Christ. When Peter was imprisoned, we read, "But the angel of the Lord by night opened the prison doors, and brought them forth" (Acts 5:19). In this instance these supernatural beings delivered the ministers of the Gospel from their bonds in prison. Again, in Acts 12, Peter had the same experience of deliverance by a heavenly visitant. Every line of evidence intelligence can pursue shows conclusively that angels are real beings, occupying a sphere of life which is at present higher than human life.

The conclusions must be, if there is a higher kind of life than man knows, there has to be at least the possibility of man's achieving this sphere where the higher life exists. Indeed, we are definitely told in the Word of God that we who have received Christ as Saviour shall some day not only enter this sphere of living but shall find ourselves in that day superior to these mighty celestial ones. "Behold, what manner of love the Father hath bestowed upon us, that we should be called the sons of God . . . " (I John 3:1).

We must also mention evidence that testifies to the reality of the dark, evil, supernatural world that is dominated by the sinister figure of the adversary. The Word of God speaks of "fallen angels." "And the angels which kept not their first estate, but left their own habitation, he hath reserved in everlasting chains under darkness unto the judgment of the great day" (Jude 1:6). Their judgment is not yet complete.

The brightest light always casts the deepest shadow and the dark side of the picture is the evidence in the spiritual world of a minor evil kingdom, a kingdom that is at present in rebellion against God and attempting to undermine the kingdom of God. This kingdom is ruled over by Satan. The program and the plans of Satan are doomed to failure. God, the infinite, omnipotent, omniscient One, could, by His unlimited authority and power, instantly crush that rebellion. But it has pleased His purpose to allow this rebellion to run its course to its predestined end, that there might be, even in heaven, a demonstration of His sovereignty.

The kingdom of Satan is the bitter enemy of man. That is why we read in Ephesians 6:12: "For we wrestle not against flesh and bood, but against principalities, against powers, against the rulers of the darkness of this world, against spiritual wickedness in high places." A clearer translation is that of J. B. Phillips, quoted here for the sake of comparison: "For our fight is not against any physical enemy; it is against organizations and powers that are spiritual. We are up against the unseen power that controls this dark world and spiritual agents from the very headquarters of evil."

Satan is on the alert to frustrate the servants of God so far as he is able. The Apostle Paul wrote to the Christians at Thessalonica, "Wherefore we would have come unto you, even I Paul, once and again; but Satan hindered us" (I Thess. 2:18).

The Holy Book depicts the entire world of man's political and natural existence as being in bondage to Satan, and the purpose of the dying of Jesus Christ was to provide a means of power by which men of this world could recover themselves from the snare and the power of Satan. "And that they may recover themselves out of the snare of the devil, who are taken captive by him at his will" (II Tim. 2:26).

The kingdom of Satan is highly organized and is remarkably powerful. We note, for instance, in the 10th chapter of Daniel that the prophet had been praying twenty-one days for help and revelation from God. On the twenty-first day there came to him the angel Gabriel, who stated that he had been on the way to answer Daniel's prayer from the day the prophet began praying. However, Gabriel said one of the princes of Satan's kingdom had met him and hindered his coming. For twenty-one days the angel of God and the emissary of Satan wrestled and Gabriel was not able to prevail until Michael, the prince of archangels, came to his aid. If the kingdom of Satan has such power that one of his emissaries could delay a messenger of God twenty-one days, what chance would a finite, weak, fallible man have in the hands of the king of this realm? None whatever. Man would be utterly undone, helpless and hopeless were it not for the fact that Jesus Christ is "greater than he that is in the world." How wonderful it is to place our confidence and trust in Jesus Christ, the overcomer. Greater is our Saviour than our enemy. More powerful, more matchless in His grace and wisdom is He who would seek our salvation than he who seeks our destruction.

In Ezekiel 28 we are told how Satan became the devil by his act of rebellion against God; and Satan, with the rebellious angels, was cast out of heaven. Evidently the place of their habitation was this earth, but unlike the earth as we know it. As a result of this assault on the supremacy of the eternal — this clash of the will of Lucifer with the will of God — a malignancy was brought into existence out of which came forth all the sin that has left in its wake the carnage of the centuries. God smote the earth — the scene of rebellion — in judgment. The earth fell into a state of sheer chaos as is recorded in Genesis 1:2. "The earth was without form, and void." Jarred from its original orbit about the sun, our earth floated in space like a black cloud, a sunless, silent thing in a funeral convoy.

*It is possible that this cataclysm put the world on its present axis, and was responsible for pulling it out of its course and changing the seasons. According to this theory an ancestral sun passed through our solar system and

---

*see *The Earth the Theater of the Universe,* by Clarence H. Benson.

struck a planet that would be where the asteroids are now. Bode's Law would seem to confirm this fact. The axis of the angle of the earth, compared with the way the asteroids broke up, draws a line as though an ancestral sun passed our planet, leaving it an empty waste, and crashed into a planet that was once where the asteroids are now. Thus, God judged those angels that kept not their first estate.

The Word of God does reveal He withdrew our planet from its chaotic state, lifted it back to its full orbit, caused the sun to shine through the encompassing darkness and reformed it as the earth of today. He created man to take the place of Satan as its prince and ruler. Later, influenced by Satan, we have the sad fact that man joined Satan's rebellion against God. He, too, broke fellowship with his Creator, and immediately the plan for man's restoration through divine redemption was initiated. The whole purpose of God now is to populate the universe with redeemed creatures at last. Scripture declares that Satan, in spite of the fact that he is judged, in spite of the fact that he was the instigator of the fall of man, is, nevertheless, king in two realms. He is over the "fallen spirits," whose name is legion, and he is also the ruler of this world order.

"And they came to Jesus, and see him that was possessed with the devil, and had the legion, sitting, and clothed, and in his right mind: and they were afraid" (Mark 5:15).

"And Jesus asked him, saying, What is thy name? And he said, Legion: because many devils were entered into him" (Luke 8:30).

The authority which Satan exercises over the hosts of demons (fallen angels) is asserted in the Word of God in many places. "Then was brought unto him one possessed with a devil, blind, and dumb; and he healed him insomuch that the blind and dumb both spake and saw" (Matt. 12:22). Satan is still king of our cosmic world. Satan is said to be the god and the prince of this world and his satanic authority is declared in Ephesians 6:12.

The Bible asserts that these demons do the will of their king. It is also revealed that they render wholehearted, willing co-operation to any satanic project. To this they were evidently committed when they left their first estate. "For . . . God spared not the angels that sinned, but cast them down to hell, and delivered them into chains of darkness, to be reserved unto judgment" (II Peter 2:4).

In considering the activities of demons, we must distinguish between demon possession or control and demon influence. In the one case, the body is entered and a dominating control is gained. In the latter case, a warfare from without is carried on by suggestion, temptation and impulse.

Investigation of the Scripture in regard to demon possession reveals that this host of fallen angels is made up of spirits that have no bodies and desire embodiment. Their power must be dependent upon embodiment. Perhaps this is part of their punishment! "When the unclean spirit is gone out of a man, he walketh through dry places, seeking rest, and findeth none. Then he saith, 'I will return into my house from whence I came out'; and when he is come, he findeth it empty, swept, and garnished. Then goeth he, and taketh with himself seven other spirits more wicked than himself, and they enter in and dwell there: and the last state of that man is worse than the first" (Matt. 12:43-45). This Scripture tells us that more than one demon can invade a man at one time. If they cannot enter the body of a mortal, they want to enter the body of a beast, as was the case in the account of the deliverance of the maniac of Gadara. The demons besought our Lord to command that they not go into the sea but be embodied by the swine.

Christians can be *influenced* by demonic, satanic suggestion, but no Christian can be demon *possessed*. He has within him the presence and the power of the Holy Spirit. "Know ye not that your body is the temple of the Holy Ghost?" (I Cor. 6:19). "Greater is he that is in you, than he that is in the world" (I John 4:4). But a believer can be disobedient to the Word of God, come under demonic influence, and lose his usability. He can become a plaything of the adversary. He can be buffeted and abused. The way to defeat the adversary in this area is to see to it that Jesus Christ controls all that you are and have and hope to be, unconditionally and forever. It is a known fact that when the devil does not appear as a roaring lion, he appears as an angel of light.

We have seen that there is a supernatural world, a vast world of celestial beings, and in direct contrast, a minor world of evil beings. And that our protection against this world of evil beings, both now and forever, is our absolute, implicit trust in the One who is the conqueror of evil — our Lord Jesus Chirst. You are not safe in this world, neither are you safe in the vast forever, unless your life is hid with Christ in God.

chapter five

CAN WE TALK WITH THE DEAD?

"There shall not be found among you anyone that . . . useth divination, or an observer of times, or an enchanter, or a witch, or a charmer, or a wizard, or a consulter with familiar spirits, or a necromancer. For all that do these things are an abomination unto the LORD . . ." (Deut. 18:10-12). "And when they shall say unto you, Seek unto them that hath familiar spirits, and unto wizards that peep, and that mutter: should not a people seek unto their God? for the living to the dead?" (Isaiah 8:19).

The whole subject of attempting to communicate with the dead through psychic research is discussed, explained, and explicitly forbidden in the Word of God. Rationalistic, liberal theologians miss all the Biblical report. They do not have an organ of receptivity to Biblical happenings. Spiritual whoredom with the philosophical trends of past and present has blinded them against the Holy Spirit's revelation.

Many believe in spiritism (communication with the dead). Scores of the most noted men in every branch of science have committed themselves to the belief that the phenomenon of talking with the dead is a reality. With

Flammarion, they believe, "Any scientific man who declares that the spiritist's phenomenon is impossible is one who speaks without knowing what he is talking about."

Mr. Sherwood Eddy, the liberal who has contributed frequently to "Christian Century," an organ advocated by the National Council of Churches, has written a book entitled, *You Will Survive After Death*. Mr. Eddy tells about startling psychic experiences that have convinced him. For example, he tells about a full daylight sitting with Mrs. Pamela Nash of London, at which five of his dead relatives were identified and twenty-eight correct details concerning them were given. Mr. Eddy tells about conversing with his late father and with General Leonard, the deceased governor of the Philippines, a childhood friend. He claims that facts were given to him that no one on earth could verify but himself. He claims to have talked with George Russell, Irish author, in which Russell described the afterlife saying, "I am here speechless amid splendor; we do not talk of heaven or hell here; it is just life abundant; nothing enchains us."

Finally, Mr. Eddy concludes his book by telling about the transportation by the aid of a medium, upon request, of a heavy, wrought-iron ash tray from a living room in Chicago to his apartment at the Sherman Square Hotel in New York City. This is known in the spiritistic world as an apport. He tells of ectoplasmic figures of tall men, short women, and children—all with widely different voices—that appeared before him and another group in the city of Philadelphia. It is my firm conviction that this coalescence with psychic phenomena is going to be the next direction of liberal theology.

There are thousands of people who claim that they can and do talk with the dead. Certainly it is a natural longing, a natural desire, for the continuance of both the personality beyond the grave and the knowledge of loved ones who have gone on before us. Who has not longed for the touch of a hand that has vanished? Who does not long for the sound of a voice that is still? The very thought of spirit communication arouses the keenest interest.

Much of this so-called phenomena is outright chicanery. The public is very often entertained by magicians who explain the tricks of the trade and treat us to stunts of their own. Thurston, Houdini, Keller and Herman were very adept at this. These men were entertainers—nothing more. Most of the professional mediums, especially the fortune tellers, have been exposed and have been proved to be nothing more than skillful deceivers. If this were not the case, then by wagering on the horses and playing the stock market, they could be millionaires over night!

The Psychical Research Society, organized in 1882 and composed of a group of eminent scholars and scientists, has been doing research work in the field of psychic phenomena. They report that to date they have found only two or possibly three mediums that did not at some time or other resort to infamous methods of deception. The Fox sisters, who initiated spiritism as a religion in the United States, at the close of their lives repudiated the whole business.

However, certainly some of the phenomena are definitely supernatural. For example, the events that Mr. Eddy relates in his book are the testimony of an undoubtedly honest man. What he saw, as far as he was concerned, really happened. Our desire is to identify the source or the power behind Mr. Eddy's experiences. Was it of God or of Satan?

The dead do not come back. According to the Word of God, we cannot communicate with the dead. There is no evidence whatsoever of previous existence (reincarnation) on the part of anyone living today.

So-called prenatal regression, or regression beyond birth by hypnosis, is an impossibility and therefore no proof of reincarnation. Its impossibility is obvious from a scientific point of view. My friend, Dr. Herbert Burrows, states:

> We know the processes of memory; we know there is an actual physical record made within the brain. When an infant is born, the brain has billions of tiny cells (14 billion) that form the basic framework for memory. Each time a new memory factor occurs, a cell will send out a connecting link or dendrite to establish contact with another cell. This dendrite is visible under the microscope. It remains unless destroyed by disease or injury, though lack of use may cause it to become weakened in function.
>
> Anatomical studies show us that these connections do not exist at birth and that they only develop as the infant is subjected to more and more stimuli by the outside world. Thus, the only physical basis of any memory is formed after birth and consists of experiences or thoughts learned after birth.
>
> There is a physical basis for all memory after birth that can be established by microscopic examination. People can be regressed by hypnosis to any age, but there is no basis for memory of actual experiences prior to birth. Such suggestions as thought transference could be considered a scientific possibility, even if the means is not understood; but the suggestion of memory for events prior to birth cannot be considered as a scientific possibility.

Anyone who purports to prove prenatal regression is being deceived, because the subject is undoubtedly receiving vague impressions from other minds by telepathy or merely recalling scenes from memory, perhaps of books read or pictures seen, etc. There is another dangerous possibility the Bible calls demon possession, which may be the explanation for these phenomena. The Bible makes the clear statement that "it is appointed unto men *once* to die, but after this the judgment" (Heb. 9:27). It teaches that men live on this earth only one time. Any exceptions to this rule are recorded in the Word of God as divine interventions for a unique and special reason. For example, Lazarus, and the son of the widow of Nain, were returned to life from death by the command of the Lord Jesus Christ as a demonstration of His deity.

Since Elijah appeared with Moses on the Mount of Transfiguration, he was obviously not John the Baptist reincarnated (Matt. 17:1-8 and Mark 9:2-8). As Jesus and His disciples were coming down from the Mount, after they had seen Elijah, His disciples asked Him, "Why then say the scribes that Elias must first come? And Jesus answered and said unto them, 'Elias truly shall first come, and restore all things'" (Matt. 17:10, 11). Jesus was referring here to the prophecy in Malachi 4:5,6: "Behold, I will send you Elijah the prophet before the coming of the great and dreadful day of the Lord: And he shall turn the heart of the fathers to the children, and the heart of the children to their fathers, lest I come and smite the earth with a curse."

Revelation 11 tells us that at the end of the tribulation period Elijah and Moses will appear in the city of Jerusalem. They will give their witness concerning Christ the Messiah and then be slain. For three and one-half days their bodies will lie on the streets of Jerusalem, after which the spirit of life from God will enter into them. When they stand upon their feet great fear will fall upon all who see it. And then, obedient to a voice out of heaven, they will ascend in a cloud as their enemies behold them.

John the Baptist had come already, and with a ministry so completely in the Spirit and power of Elijah's future ministry (Luke 1:17) that in a prophetic and typical sense it could be said, "Elias is come already." The angel told Zacharias, "And he shall go before Him in the spirit and power of Elias, to turn the hearts of the fathers to the children, and the disobedient to the wisdom of the just; to make ready a people prepared for the Lord (Luke 1:17,18).

There is no more powerful Scripture to disprove reincarnation than that of the transfiguration. This demonstrates the eternal continuity of personality. Moses and Elijah, after two thousand years, made an appearance on the Mount of Transfiguration with Christ. Those who were resurrected always came back in bodily form, never as disembodied spirits. When Lazarus came forth from the dead, his lips were sealed concerning the four days he was absent from his loved ones. When the righteous dead came from their graves on the day that Jesus Christ was crucified, they came back without saying one word. Their lips and minds were sealed with regard to what was on the other side. I am sure that all that happened on the other side was blotted from their memories. Paul, the apostle, was caught up into the third heaven and saw things he himself said were "unlawful to utter."

Perhaps no Scripture bearing on the spirit world is more misunderstood than the story of King Saul and the witch of Endor. The spiritists revel in telling about that incident and base their whole theology on the fact that Samuel communicated with Saul, as do the reincarnationists. However, they deny all doctrinal truth of the Christian faith. Spiritism is the antithesis to Christianity.

The Bible everywhere condemns anything that the spiritists practice and everything that the spiritists and reincarnationists preach and teach. Apart from this one incident in the Word of God, in which Samuel purportedly appeared to reiterate the doom that had already been promised to Saul, there is no other similar record in the Scripture.

In I Samuel 28 this exciting Old Testament tragedy unfolds. Samuel, the prophet, was dead. Saul had gone from bad to worse. His spiritual deterioration was now complete. Mad with jealousy, swallowed up by envy, frustration, and ambition, he had fallen from his plane of splendid possibilities as a king. His soul was yielded to hatred and its final fruit, murder. Abandoning the mind and will of God, he had followed his own rule and leaned to his own understanding—the victim of his lusts and desires. Though previously warned of the disaster that would befall him, he had turned his back on God and God released him to an awful fate.

Saul was surrounded by his enemies. The Philistines were marshalling their hosts against him. With an agitated mind and heart, he contemplated the coming morrow, the impending conflict. He was apprehensive, filled with fear and despair. The priests could give him no wisdom. He felt himself cut off from the life of God. Then he thought of Samuel: "If Samuel were alive, I could seek his counsel. Why not seek it now?" He also remembered that he himself, by the dictum of the Spirit of God, had sent out an edict that anyone in Israel who had a familiar spirit, those who were mediums, wizards or necromancers, and who were caught in the practice of these things, would be put to death.

The Bible defines a medium as one who claims to relay messages from the dead to the living. A wizard is one who is supposed to know all about what is beyond this world. Such a practice is related specifically to astrology. A necromancer is one who communicates with the dead. These are the Scriptural definitions, and they are generally accepted today.

Saul had issued the edict. Practices in the occult were prohibited by the law of God under penalty of death. But as soon as the desire to speak to Samuel was in Saul's mind, he made known his wish to find a medium. Cautiously they told him of a woman who had a familiar spirit, or a "control," as they are called today, a medium who lived in the rocks of Endor. He determined to go to see her and to use her powers. That is how low he had fallen; how spiritually destitute he had become. He was making himself a willing instrument, not only to violate the law of God but to violate his own enforcement of that law. He was trampling upon his own dignity and honor and was willing to shame himself in the presence of the men before whom, in the past, he had tried to maintain an image of righteousness and faithfulness.

When Saul went to see the witch of Endor, he disguised himself and took two companions with him. They mounted their horses, rode through that eerie night, and forced their way up the rocky defile to the cave where the woman dwelt. Ears that were alert could have heard the hoofs of the horses ring out on that fearful night. As Saul reached there, he saw a light in the crevice and the woman opened the door. Saul went through the doors of that cave. In the presence of King Saul she shrank back, but evidently did not know who he was.

The king bent from his great height and told her his errand and asked that she might bring up from the dead one that he would name to her. She protested, saying, "Don't you know that King Saul has issued an edict ordering all that have a familiar spirit to be put to death?" Not recognizing Saul, she thought someone had come to spy out her life and she would not lend herself to her own destruction.

The king swore by the Lord God of Israel that no harm would come to her, and then asked her to bring Samuel, the prophet, back from the dead.

She expected to go into a trance, and what is the supposedly controlling spirit would then make use of her organs of speech like a ventriloquist, impersonate Samuel and deceive Saul. Suddenly she gave a shriek as she saw a spirit rise like a wraith from the earth, an accusing thing, dreadful and terrible in its mysterious silence. The woman was overcome with horror. She had played her game of deception for many years and was familiar with a particular spirit; but this spirit she did not know. Shivering with terror, she cried out, "Why hast thou deceived me? for thou art Saul!"

The king told her not to be afraid and to tell him all that she saw. She told him she saw gods rising out of the earth. To her frightened vision there were many. Intent upon his one obsession and thinking of only one person— Samuel—the king inquired of the woman what form the apparition had.

She answered that she saw an old man coming up, covered with a mantle. Saul himself perceived it was Samuel and stooping low before him, listened to the voice that came from him. From that moment all the conversation was between Saul and "the old man." The woman has no relation to it. She became a mere spectator. Samuel seemed actually to come back. It was an amazing spectacle. The dimness, the shadows of the cave, the flickering light of the lamp made the mystery all the more intense. There Saul bowed—shivering, trembling and shaking—to hear once again what he had previously heard, reiterated in what he thought was the voice of Samuel, the words of his own doom. At length he fell upon the floor of the cave in such great distress that the woman tried to help him. Recovering, he took a little food and then, with his companions, rode away into the night.

It is to be noted that no revelation was given that had not already been given. He was told merely what Samuel had said in life, that the kingdom was to be rent from him and given to David, that his armies were to be put to flight and that Saul himself was to be slain. Thus Samuel appeared to have come back.

But the Word of God says, "So Saul died for his transgressions which he committed against the Lord, even against the word of the Lord, which he kept not, and also for asking counsel of one that had a familiar spirit, to inquire of it; *And inquired not of the Lord:* therefore he slew him, and turned the kingdom unto David the son of Jesse" (I Chron. 10:13-14). Here is the definite statement that this woman did not communicate with the dead but with a demon.

The death of Saul, rather than an argument *for* talking with the dead, is a dynamic denunciation of God *against* those who seek to have communication with the dead. Saul's death was God's reaffirmation of His law against seeking to speak with the dead, and a terrifying witness of God's integrity behind His law. Samuel did not come back; an evil spirit impersonated him. The fact that the woman was seized with terror makes us realize that what happened was out of the realm of her usual rigmarole. If contact is ever claimed with the dead, it must be accounted for by this explanation.

C. S. Lewis says, "There are two equal and opposite errors into which our race can fall about the devils. One is to disbelieve in their existence. The other is to believe and to feel an excessive and unhealthy interest in them."

There is indeed a solemn reality repeatedly found in the Scriptures that clearly reveals the intrusion of fallen spirits into the cosmos and that such an intrusion is natural, since Satan is the one who has brought the cosmos to its present form because of the ravages of sin (see Matt. 8:28-34; Matt. 9:32,33; Acts 8:6-8; Acts 16; Acts 19:15,16; James 2:19, etc.).

A physician friend of mine, a devout Christian, former U.S.N. psychiatrist and at one time chief surgeon of the Mercy Hospital in San Diego, told me that he had witnessed demon possession in our culture many times. He had seen men and women delivered and set free in the name of Jesus Christ. He said he had actually demonstrated this before his colleagues who do not believe that such a thing is possible, and they offered no explanation.

No one can anticipate the relief that will come to the universe when the Scripture is fulfilled that promises a day when Christ will put down all rule, power and authority. "The kingdoms of this world are become the kingdoms of our Lord, and of his Christ . . ." (Rev. 11:15).

It has been a revealing truth that whenever these people come back, supposedly from the dead, by the impersonation the demon makes, they immediately vanish if they are rebuked in the name of Jesus Christ. Dr. A. C. Dixon says, "Spiritism is a planned and determined overthrow of the Christian faith."

There has never been a spiritist who believed in the plenary inspiration of the Scriptures, in the deity of our Lord Jesus Christ, in His atonement on the cross for the world's sin, the fact of His resurrection from the dead, and the truth that men are saved through Him. A spiritist's séance can be broken up when one begins to proclaim the majesty of Christ, the person of His deity, and the glory of His finished, atoning work on the cross. Sir A. Conan Doyle said: "The whole doctrine of original sin, the fall, the vicarious atonement, the placation of the Almighty by blood, all this is abhorrent to me. The spirit guides do not insist upon these aspects of religion."

Shortly after I had conducted the funeral service for her husband, a widow, severely distraught, came to see me. She said, "I have never believed in spiritism, but the other night I was home alone. As you know, my heart has been broken in the loss of my husband. Suddenly, in the shadows of that room he stood before me. We carried on a conversation together. It was the strangest thing that ever happened to me. It happened the next night and the night after that. It happened so often I began to look forward to it. He tells me that all the things I have believed are not true. He tells me that it is altogether different from what the Word of God says and I am in a terrible state. What is this? What is going on?"

I replied, "I want you to do one thing. The next time you think that your husband is there and you think you are having communication with him, ask him if he comes in the name of Jesus Christ. Ask him if he believes that Jesus Christ died on the cross for his sins and tell him that if he is not saved by faith in Christ, he must be lost. Talk about Christ to him, and see what happens."

She reported later that the séance happened again. She asked the exact questions I had suggested, and he disappeared instantly. She never saw the so-called materialization of her husband again. It was not her husband with whom she was talking; her husband is with the Lord. It was a demon! It was this very thing we have been discussing—demon impersonation.

God tells us in no uncertain language that we are not to have anything to do with mediums, necromancers, clairvoyants, astrologers and all who deal with familiar spirits or attempt to know what is not already written in the Word of God.

In a score of places He speaks in the livid thunder of indignation against this unholy business. Even attempting to talk with the dead is unlawful. God hates it because it is demonism. Leviticus 20:6 says: "And the soul that turneth after such as have familiar spirits, and after wizards, to go a whoring after them, I will even set my face against that soul, and will cut him off from among his people." Again, "A man also or a woman that hath a familiar spirit (a medium), or that is a wizard, shall surely be put to death: they shall stone them with stones: their blood shall be upon them" (Lev. 20:27). God commanded that anyone who gave himself to be the agent of a demon should be eliminated from the society of Israel by death. We have to proclaim victory through Jesus Christ over all powers of darkness.

Talking with the dead is not only unlawful and dangerous, it is unnecessary. Most of the erstwhile messages are puerile. Sir Oliver Lodge's son talked about the kind of cigars they had in the celestial world! The Bible gives us all the assurance that we need as far as the future life is concerned. If you have not placed your faith and confidence in the Word of God, you are not enjoying the Scripture that says, "Blessed are they that have not seen, and yet have believed." It is not expected that we shall understand all about the infinite and all about the unseen world. God expects us to exercise faith with regard to the future life. One can ratify his curiosity in the séance room, but it will be at the expense of his faith. It can victimize him into a living death.

The record of only three case histories out of many, taken from *Heresies Exposed,* by William C. Irvine, ought to serve as a grave warning. Mr. Reader Harris tells us the first one. "The most remarkable case of mediumship I have ever met with was that of a young lady who commenced with a little—seemingly innocent—table turning at a children's party and finished up by death in a mad house."

The second case is described by Mr. F. Swanson. "A woman's husband came into contact with spiritism. Up to this time he was all that could be desired. When he took to spiritism, he came in touch with a certain spiritist woman who claimed affinity. The result was this: The man cruelly deserted his wife and left her to die of a broken heart. That man today is passing as a leading official of the spiritist circle in England."

Here is a third case. As a young man, Mr. Reader Harris went with his father to the house of Dr. Gully, a leading spiritist in Malvern, where Mr. Home, the great spiritist writer and lecturer, lay dying. He tells how they went to make Mr. Home's will, but found it impossible to proceed "because of the rapping of the spirits and the general turmoil among the furniture of the room." Demons were already there in all their power to claim their victim who had long before yielded to them.

Beattie Crozier, M.D. says: "Three of my friends, men of eminence who really believe in spiritism, have told me they have forbidden the very name of it in their homes as if it were a thing accursed, because by the black magic which is always a part of it, it so often leads to insanity and death."

The Bible tells us all we need to know about the condition of our loved ones in the other life. If God had meant us to know more than we do, He would have revealed it to us in His Word. We know enough from the Word of God about the wonderful celestial land being prepared by the hands of the One who flung the worlds into space and dotted the blue heavens with their starry diamonds. We know enough to be comforted in the hour of sorrow, to realize that if our loved ones fall asleep in Jesus Christ, they are in the radiant society of the redeemed; and Jesus Christ, the matchless Saviour, who broke sin's power on Calvary's cross, is their eternal King. He said: "In my Father's house are many mansions: if it were not so, I would have told you. I go to prepare a place for you. And if I go and prepare a place for you, I will come again, and receive you unto myself; that where I am, there ye may be also" (John 14:2,3).

I know of no other Scripture that intrigues me more than "Eye hath not seen, nor ear heard, neither have entered into the heart of man, the things which God hath prepared for them that love him (I Cor. 2:9). I beheld one of the most gorgeous sights ever my privilege to see when flying over the Grand Canyon early one morning. As the sun was rising, it seemed to light on the Canyon for hundreds of miles with a magnificence that beggars description. It was beautiful but the Word of God says: "Eye hath not seen. . . . " I've heard music so rapturous that it almost seemed as though I was transported to the heavenlies, but again the Word of God says, "Nor ear heard, neither have entered into the heart of man, the things which God hath prepared for them that love Him."

In Him, you will find all the serenity and security that an aching soul will ever require for all the endless eons of eternity. How much better this than the poor, miserable work of the darkened séance room.

In the story of the rich man and Lazarus, Dives, the rich man, found himself in Hades. He called to Abraham and begged him to send Lazarus to his five brothers on earth. He said: "Lest they also come into this place of torment." Abraham replied to Dives, "They have Moses and the prophets; let them hear them" (Luke 16:28,29).

"Nay, Father Abraham:" said Dives, "but if one went unto them from the dead, they will repent" (Luke 16:30).

A man once said to me: "If somebody came back from the dead and told me about the other world, I would believe it."

I replied: "One did come back from the dead, and He did tell us all about it and His name is Jesus Christ. On the morning of the third day the breath of God swept through the clay, and Jesus Christ, the monument to the power of God, stood alive before the open tomb—the resurrected God."

The fact of the physical resurrection of Jesus Christ is absolutely the keystone in the arch of Christian revelation. The physical, bodily resurrection of Jesus Christ is an attested fact of history. He did come back. He came back to tell us that He has conquered death, conquered the grave. The tomb is no longer a blind alley; it is a thoroughfare that closes with the twilight to open with the dawn. He went to the cross in your stead and mine. He broke this power called sin that alienated us from God. In the majesty of divine language, "He bore in His body our sins on the accursed tree." He said, "He that believeth in Me shall never die."

David said that the dead cannot come to us but one day, in God's providence, we will go to them. How blessed is the truth that it is the way of the cross that leads home.

There is only one way that will take you safely from

this world into the next one. That one way is through faith in the Christ who came from that world to us and who went back into that world to prepare a place for you and for me. We all desire the touch of the hand now vanished, the sound of the voice now stilled, and one day, by the promise of this matchless Christ, we shall be with those who have gone on ahead, in His love forever and forever.

Christ alone came back from the gate and the grave of death to assure us:

> *"There is a land of pure delight,*
> *Where saints immortal reign;*
> *Infinite day excludes the night,*
> *And pleasures banish pain."*

Many people think the most wonderful part of Christianity is the prospect of that eternal world with the Saviour where there will be no disease, no sin, and no death. But actually, with Him there is a lot of heaven here in this world right now.

Spiritism is something to be greatly feared, something that no Bible-believing Christian, for the sake of his own soul, his own testimony, should have anything to do with. Fear it as you would the yawning door of hell itself and stay as far away from it as possible. If it were for us to know more, God would have told us; but in His great wisdom He knows best. When we enter that glorious world He is preparing for those who love Him and serve Him, I am sure we shall say with the Queen of Sheba, as she was overawed by the magnificence of Solomon's splendors, "The half has not been told me!" How much better this prospect than dingy, dark rooms where deceived people hold communications with demons and have as their future a hell without light and without Christ.

chapter six

WHERE ARE THE DEAD?

"Man dieth . . . and where is he" (Job 14:10)?

"Today shalt thou be with me in paradise" (Luke 23:43).

Cannon Henry Parry Liddon, an Anglican scholar, tells of an old military officer who, having returned from India, was relating to a group of friends the story of the Indian mutiny. His audience hung in breathless interest on his words. Suddenly he stopped, and as they waited for his next word, he quietly continued, "I expect some day to see something much more wonderful than that."

His friends were surprised. He was an old man past seventy years; and because he was retired from active duty in the army, they felt his traveling days were over. So they said, "Something more wonderful than that? Where? And When?"

He thoughtfully answered, "I mean in the first five minutes after death."

The first five minutes after death! What would he see? Where would he be? Do we *know* where he would be? Do we *know* what he would see? What would the first five minutes mean to him, or to you or to me?

The question, "Where are the dead?" is the universal question of the ages. Like Banquo's ghost, it will not down.

Once Andrew Carnegie offered a million dollars to anyone who could prove to his satisfaction the reality of a life beyond this one. Some shallow-minded agnostic in the city of Toledo, Ohio, was laughing at the Church because of her seeming impotency to furnish this proof. "I marvel," he said, "that all the ministers in Christendom do not rush to Carnegie's store and claim the prize. Is the Church so rich that she does not need the money; or is she so poor in faith that she does not dare accept the offer; or is it because all the priests and preachers are hypocrites, offering something for which they know they cannot furnish any proof?"

What this infidel did not seem to realize is that the only textbook on this subject is the Bible. And if you do not accept what it has to say, there is no other authority, no other absolute source of knowledge. To burn out your eyes and then offer a huge reward for light, gives guarantee only of continued darkness. To throw away the only textbook on the subject means to know nothing about the subject. I am so glad that God did not confuse us. He gave us only one revelation of Himself; that revelation is twofold: the *living Word,* the Lord Jesus Christ, and the *written Word,* the Bible. There is no other revelation.

All time in the United States is based on U. S. Naval Observatory time. The time for Europe is set in Geneva. The ultimate authority for all the time pieces is the stars. Reject the stars and you can never be sure your watch is correct. The one authority on all spiritual matters, including man's immortality, is the Bible. What the stars are to time the Bible is to spiritual knowledge.

Some people are quite ready to believe there is a heaven for the righteous, but that there is no such place as hell for the Christ-rejector. The truth is there is more in the Bible about hell than there is about heaven.

At one time Robert Ingersoll was delivering his famous lecture on hell. He called hell the "scarecrow of religion." He told his audience how unscientific hell was, how all intelligent people had decided there was no such place. Suddenly an inebriated fellow came to the front and said, "Bob, I liked your lecture; I liked what you said about hell; but Bob, I want you to be sure about it, because I'm depending on you."

Where do we go from here? Lazarus was carried by the angels into Abraham's bosom but where is that? In torment, the rich man lifted up his eyes in Hades, but where is that? The penitent thief went directly to Paradise from the cross, to meet the Saviour, but where is that? Judas went to his own place but where is that? These questions take us beyond the range of mere human investigation. Answers may be inferred from rationalization, philosophy and para psychology, but they will never be satisfying apart from divine revelation. The right answers must be revealed by the Holy Spirit. This is our authority: the sure testimony of the eternal Word of God.

It was Dr. W. E. Beiderwolf who said that the destructive critic of the Bible always reminded him of the story of an Irish highway robber named Pat. He pulled his gun on a man and said, "Your money or your life."

The man answered, "I'll tell you what I'll do. I'll give you all the money I've got for that gun."

"Sure," said Pat, "it's an even trade."

When the swap was made, the man said, "Now, you hand back that money, or I'll blow your brains out."

"Well, bedad, you can blow away," replied Pat, "there's never a devil of a bit of powder in the old thing!"

In the same way these would-be destroyers of the Bible rush upon us with weapons that are never loaded. Modernism has failed and is dying in the vacuum of its own denials. Today it is moving into a compromise position known as neo-orthodoxy—the same old modernism in a new robe. We hear much today about the so-called modern mind, but if a man desires to know anything concerning the future of his soul and its relation to an endless eternity, if he would have the deepest questions of his soul answered, he will find the answers in God's living Word. It is contemporary to every hour, adequate to every experience, and true in every word.

> *"Hammer away, ye rebel bands,*
> *Your hammers break,*
> *God's anvil stands."*

When Jesus died on the cross, He did not go back to heaven at once. This is made plain by His words to Mary Magdalene on the morning of His resurrection, when He said to her, "Touch me not; for I am not yet ascended to my Father" (John 20:17). That our Lord went to Paradise is evidenced by His statement to the thief who died with Him: "Today shalt thou be with me in Paradise" (Luke 23:43). What a day for the dying thief! A condemned malefactor in the forenoon, a railing blasphemer in the afternoon, a redeemed man in Paradise before sundown.

But where is Paradise?

Paradise is a Greek word used to denote the dwelling place of the righteous dead. It is the upper part of Hades.

But where is Hades?

Hades is a Greek word formerly used to denote the dwelling place of the souls of the dead in general, both good and bad, righteous and unrighteous. It is the same word as "Sheol" in Hebrew.

Hades had two compartments: the lower part for the wicked dead and the upper part (Paradise) for the righteous dead. When Jesus died, He took the penitent thief with Him into the Paradise section of Hades.

Paradise is not heaven.

Heaven is where the throne of God is. It is where God the Father is, and to this place Jesus told Mary He had not as yet ascended. Jesus went to heaven forty days after His resurrection. When He ascended two angels stood by the wondering disciples and said, "Ye men of Galilee, why stand ye gazing up into heaven? this same Jesus, which is taken up from you into heaven, shall so come in like manner as ye have seen him go into heaven" (Acts 1:11).

When Jesus went to heaven He did not go alone. He took not only the redeemed thief with Him but He took a multitude of other people as well. Quoting Psalm 68:18, Paul tells us in Ephesians 4:8: "When He ascended on high, He led captivity captive—He led a train of vanquished foes . . . " (Amp. N. T.). These captives were the

Old Testament saints who were waiting in Paradise for the finished work of Christ on the cross so that on the basis of that finished work they could be admitted to the presence of God. Zechariah 9:12 refers to these saints as "prisoners of hope." Jesus referred in some measure to the liberation of these when, quoting Isaiah 61:1, He said, "He hath sent me . . . to proclaim liberty to the captives, and the opening of the prison to them that are bound." The Scripture clearly states in Ephesians 4:8-10 that before Christ ascended into heaven, "He also descended first into the lower parts of the earth." All the saints who died before the ascension of Christ went to Paradise, the glorious part of Hades. But now Paradise is empty.

What about the Christian who dies today? His soul goes immediately to be with Christ in heaven. Two verses make this clear. Paul said: "For I am in a strait betwixt two, a desire to depart, and to be with Christ; which is far better" (Phil. 1:23). "We are confident, I say, and willing rather to be absent from the body, and to be present with the Lord" (II Cor. 5:8). These two verses settle the matter. To be absent from the body is to be present with the Lord. Since our Lord is gone into heaven, that, too, is to be the Christian's glorious destination when he says "farewell" to the friends and dear ones of this earth. His next consciousness is in the presence of our Lord Jesus Christ. There is no going to the Old Testament Paradise, no waiting in Hades. The old catechism is right when it says, "The souls of believers do immediately pass into glory." Stephen, when he was stoned, looked steadfastly up into heaven and saw Jesus standing, waiting to receive him as he cried, "Lord Jesus, receive my spirit." Jesus *stood* to receive the first Christian martyr!

Throughout the Old Testament period, until the ascension of the Lord Jesus Christ, the souls of both the believers and the unbelievers were spoken of as "going down"—going down into Hades, or Sheol. So we have Dives in the lower part of Hades calling to Lazarus in the upper part, sometimes called "Abraham's bosom." However, while the souls of the wicked are still spoken of as going down (into Hades), the souls of the saints are always spoken of as going up (into heaven) since the ascension of the Lord Jesus Christ.

Which way is up? If we say it is in the direction at right angles with the earth's surface, wherever we may happen to be, then it would be in a different direction from every point on the earth. From North America and from China it would be in exactly opposite directions. According to this, "up" would be everywhere in general and nowhere in particular.

The Word of God, speaking of the rebellion of Lucifer, tells us that he said, "I will ascend into heaven, I will exalt my throne above the stars of God: I will sit also upon the mount of the congregation, in the sides of the north: I will ascend above the heights of the clouds; I will be like the most High" (Isa. 14:13,14). Here we are informed that heaven is in the "sides of the north," and that it is above the heights of the clouds and above the stars. What is the meaning of the words "in the sides of the north"? The Revised Version reads, "In the upper most, utter most part of the north."

God says in Psalm 75:2-7: "When I shall receive the

congregation I will judge uprightly. The earth and all the inhabitants thereof are dissolved: I bear up the pillars of it. I said unto the fools, Deal not foolishly: and to the wicked, Lift not up the horn: Lift not up your horn on high: speak not with a stiff neck. For promotion cometh neither from the east, nor from the west, nor from the south. But God is the judge." It is implied that the throne of God, where He receives the congregation and judges uprightly, is in the north, since it is not in the east, the west, or the south.

North is the same direction from every point on the earth's surface, and north is "up" from everywhere. It is the same from China as from America, from the Antarctic as from the Arctic. How significant too, that the geographic and magnetic poles of the earth are always kept pointing north. Who can tell why the magnetic needle in a compass points toward the North Star? I believe it is a testimony to God's presence. When "the glory of Jehovah" visited the prophet Ezekiel, it came with a whirlwind "out of the north" (Ezek. 1:4-28). Job 26:7 tells us: "He stretcheth out the north over the empty place, and hangeth the earth upon nothing." In the northern heavens the telescopic camera reveals an apparently empty space where there are fewer stars, though the region all around is thickly dotted with them. Thus astronomers have confirmed this fascinating "rift in the sky."

Dr. R. A. Torrey believed that the moment a believer dies, he is thrust out through space, through the empty place in the north and into the presence of Jesus Christ; that this was the way into the third heaven where Christ is.

Paul tells us in II Corinthians 12:2-4 that he was

caught up into the third heaven, which he called Paradise, and saw things "not lawful for a man to utter." There is also a New Testament Paradise, not to be confused with the former Paradise part of Hades or Sheol, which is called "the paradise of God" in Revelation 2:7, and which is the same place we have in mind when we speak of heaven. This is the destination of the soul of the believer.

Today, in this age, as in the past, the souls of the Christ-rejectors go to Hades and there they will remain until the final judgment. Then they shall be resurrected and judged before the "great white throne," which for them is the resurrection of condemnation.

There are three false arguments disproved by the clear teaching of the Word of God. One is the idea of soul sleeping. Seventh-Day Adventists and others believe the soul sleeps in the grave until the resurrection. They believe that the state to which we are reduced by death is one of silence, inactivity and entire unconsciousness. But when the rich man, who "fared sumptuously," cried out in Hades, "I am tormented in this flame," most certainly *his* soul was *not* in a state of "entire unconsciousness."

Jesus, on the cross, said to the penitent thief, "Today shalt thou be with me in paradise." A moment later He said, "Father, into thy hands I commend my spirit." Thus the spirit of Jesus, as well as the spirit of the penitent thief, passed into Paradise under the care of God, while their bodies a little later were committed to the earth. It is the body that sleeps, not the soul.

The word "dead," as used in the Scriptures, does not always apply to the body. The unregenerate are spoken of as dead. "And you hath he quickened, (animated, made to live) who were dead in trespasses and sins" (Eph. 2:1). When the Prodigal Son came home, his father said, "This my son was dead, and is alive again . . ." (Luke 15:24). The Apostle Paul in writing to Timothy said, "She that liveth in pleasure is dead while she liveth" (I Tim. 5:6). In these passages we see that death does not mean non-existence or unconsciousness, but that there is a sense in which a person may be said to be dead and yet have a conscious existence. Death is not the terminus of a man's existence; it is only a transition, a station along the way.

The death of the believer is described as "falling asleep," but the sleep has reference to the body only. The fact that the soul lives and is conscious after death is plain from Matthew 10:28: "And fear not them which kill the body, but are not able to kill the soul." The body can be killed but the soul cannot. Jesus said concerning Lazarus that he was dead. But He spoke of death as a sleep, for He said, "I go, that I may awake him out of sleep" (John 11:11), which He did by raising his body from the grave.

In Matthew 27:52 it is recorded that after the resurrection of Jesus, "many bodies of the saints which slept arose." The word "bodies" implies that "slept" refers to them and not to the souls of the dead. Otherwise the word "body" would have been omitted and it would have read, "Many of the saints which slept arose."

In Acts 7:54-60 we have the account of the death of Stephen. We are told, as a result of the stoning, he "fell asleep;" that is, he died. But the words "fell asleep" cannot mean that Stephen's soul passed into a state of unconsciousness, for in verse 55 we read that "he, being full of the Holy Ghost, looked up steadfastly into heaven, and saw the glory of God, and Jesus standing on the right hand of God." And as he died Stephen said, "Lord Jesus, receive my spirit." There would be no need for such a prayer if the soul at death passes into a state of unconsciousness.

In a similar manner our dying Lord yielded up His spirit to God; that is, He permitted it to depart from His body, which afterward was taken down from the cross and buried. In Acts 13:36 it is said of King David that after he had served his generation by the will of God, he "fell on sleep," and was "laid unto his fathers, and saw corruption." That this corruption, or decay, refers only to David's body, is confirmed by what follows in the next verse: "But he (the Lord Jesus Christ) whom God raised again, saw no corruption." His soul did not sleep during the three days His body lay in Joseph's tomb. While the body of Christ was still on the cross, His soul immediately went to Paradise to meet the soul of the penitent thief, as He promised.

Jesus, before He ascended into heaven, descended into the lower parts of the earth, that is, the "underworld." That must have occurred between His death and resurrection, for it was at that time that He fulfilled His promise to meet the penitent thief in the "Paradise" section of the "underworld" and not, at some time still future. While the bodies of Jesus and the penitent thief still hung on their respective crosses, their spirits were in communion in Paradise. Christ was "the firstfruits of them that slept" (I Cor. 15:20). Here "sleep" clearly refers to the body and not the soul, for it is the resurrection of the body that the Apostle is talking about in this chapter.

The appearance of Moses and Elijah, talking with the Lord Jesus Christ in the Transfiguration, is additional proof that the soul is alive and conscious after the death of the body. Also, we are reminded how the Lord Jesus said to the Sadducees that He is not the God of the dead but the God of the living—the God of Abraham, Isaac and Jacob—and He speaks of them as being alive at that moment.

The following Scriptures are used erroneously to teach soul sleep. "For in death there is no remembrance of thee: in the grave who shall give thee thanks?" (Psalm 6:5). "The dead know not anything" (Eccles. 9:5). "Whatsoever thy hand findeth to do, do it with thy might; for there is no work, nor device, nor knowledge, nor wisdom, in the grave, whither thou goest" (Eccles. 9:10). However, the contexts of these passages show that the writer was balancing the temporal benefits of living, with their loss by dying; naturally, a dead man knows nothing of the affairs of this world—neither does the soul that has departed to another sphere of existence.

Whatever we are going to do in the name of our Lord Jesus Christ and for the glory of God must be done now, for in the grave nothing more can be done. Death breaks the connection and cuts off all communication between this world and the next.

The key to understanding the book of Ecclesiastes is found in the phrase "under the sun." Solomon was giving his estimate of life from a temporal, earthly viewpoint and declared that "under the sun" all things were futile.

To die *was* the end of earthly knowledge. But he "rises above the sun" in the last chapter, and sees things from a heavenly viewpoint, and concludes, "Then shall the dust (the body) return to the earth as it was: and the spirit shall return unto God who gave it" (Eccles. 12:7). So this teaches that it is only the body that goes into the grave and that the spirit returns to God. The very book that is used to substantiate the idea of soul sleeping actually refutes the argument.

In the case of the son of the widow of Zarephath, whom Elijah raised from the dead, Elijah prayed, "Oh Lord my God, I pray thee, let this child's soul come into him again . . . and the soul of the child came into him again, and he (his body) revived (I Kings 17:21,22).

When Jesus raised the daughter of Jairus, we read, "Her spirit came again" (Luke 8:49-56). That is, it returned to her body. If there is to be a resurrection of the body, the "soul" and "spirit" must be somewhere waiting to re-inhabit that body.

Another commonly taught error is that the wicked dead are annihilated. This is the fallacy that the soul of the wicked ceases to exist in the moment of death. This view is based on a wrong interpretation of the word "destruction." If the wicked are destroyed at death, *then* there is no such thing as the resurrection and judgment of the wicked dead; as clearly taught in the Scriptures. If they have been annihilated, they cannot be resurrected. If they are annihilated, what is the point of resurrecting them? "Marvel not at this: for the hour is coming, in which all that are in the graves shall hear his voice, And shall come forth; they that have done good, unto the resurrection of life; and they that have done evil, unto the resurrection of damnation" (John 5:28,29).

"And I saw the dead, small and great, stand before God; and the books were opened: and another book was opened, which is the book of life: and the dead were judged out of those things which were written in the books, according to their works.

"And the sea gave up the dead which were in it; and death and hell delivered up the dead which were in them: and they were judged every man according to their works.

"And death and hell were cast into the lake of fire. This is the second death.

"And whosoever was not found written in the book of life was cast into the lake of fire" (Rev. 20:12-15).

We know from Luke 16:19-31 that the rich man was alive, though his body had been buried in the earth. Judas died, as to his body, but his soul went to its own place (Acts 1:25). We are told that endless punishment awaits the wicked (Matt. 25:46), but annihilation would not be endless punishment, or any punishment at all. The "fallen angels" were not annihilated. They are now in a place of waiting to be judged (Jude 6).

There is no such thing as annihilation in nature. (See chapter one.) The servants of Pharaoh said to him, " . . . Knowest thou not yet that Egypt is destroyed?" (Exodus 10:7). But Egypt exists today. Jesus said, "Destroy this temple, and in three days I will raise it up (John 2:18-22). He meant the "temple of His body;" and though they destroyed it by crucifixion, He raised it up on the third day. In speaking of Judas, Jesus said, ". . . good were it for that man if he had never been born" (Mark

14:21). He could not be annihilated once he had been born.

The Roman Catholic Church teaches that the soul of the dying saint must be purified through its own expiatory suffering in the fires of purgatory before it is fit for heaven. Whether that soul is ever released from purgatory and allowed to enter the Paradise of God depends altogether on the number of prayers that are made for it and the amount of money given on its behalf by the living relatives. When I was a seminary student in Philadelphia, the Catholic church in that area offered for sale an insurance policy on purgatory and sold it in the churches.

Purgatory is not in the Word of God. The blood of Jesus Christ cleanses us from *all sin*. There is no need of purgatorial fires for the child of God when he has once been redeemed. As Peter said, "Not by silver or gold, but with the precious blood of Christ . . . " (I Peter 1:18,19). Christ's vicarious death on the cross is adequate for all our unforgiven sin, our unconquered present, and our uncertain future.

> *Jesus paid it all,*
> *All to Him I owe.*
> *Sin had left a crimson stain*
> *He washed it white as snow.*

There is no purgatory. If you have trusted in Him, you go to be with Him. The only way you can have a title to God's presence is to know that you have been born again. "Therefore if any man be in Christ, he is a new creature; old things are passed away; behold, all things are become new" (II Cor. 5:17).

The 15th chapter of I Corinthians describes the resurrection of the body. The natural body, which is buried, is to be raised a spiritual body. What the nature of the spiritual body is we do not yet know, but one day we shall! However, we do know this much: our resurrection body is to be like that of our Lord Jesus Christ. We remember that in His post-resurrection body He was no longer limited to a time, space, material world. He moved in a dimension that we know exists but that we do not yet comprehend. He passed through doors that were shut and locked. And "we shall be like Him!"

Our resurrected, glorified body will not be a body of flesh and blood, for the Bible says, "Flesh and blood cannot inherit the kingdom of God." But the body will be one of flesh and bone, like Christ's glorified body. The glorified body of Christ was bloodless and our resurrection body will have no blood because there will be no need of it. The purpose of the blood in our present body is to supply nourishment to wasting cells that are in constant need of repair. Where there is no wasting of body cells and tissue, there is no need of blood.

In his vision John reveals to us that in heaven the inhabitants "shall neither hunger nor thirst." There shall be no more sickness or death, and there will be no night there. Food is for the purpose of supplying nourishment to a wasting body. Sickness is a sign of a wasting body, and night is for the purpose of sleep and rest, recuperating a wasting body. Since none of these are going to have any place in heaven, there is no need to supply nourishment. The resurrection body will be an eternal body, incorruptible and undefiled that will never fade away. In that body we shall dwell forever in the dazzling light of our Lord's presence. We shall sing the song which none but the redeemed of earth can sing.

> And they sung a new song, saying, Thou are worthy to take the book, and to open the seals thereof: for thou wast slain, and hast redeemed us to God by thy blood out of every kindred, and tongue, and people, and nation;
> And hast made us unto our God kings and priests: and we shall reign on the earth.
> And I beheld, and I heard the voice of many angels round about the throne and the beasts and the elders: and the number of them was ten thousand times ten thousand, and thousands of thousands;
> Saying with a loud voice, Worthy is the Lamb that was slain to receive power, and riches, and wisdom, and strength, and honour, and glory, and blessing.
> And every creature which is in heaven, and on earth, and under the earth, and such as are in the sea, and all that are in them, heard I saying, Blessing, and honour, and glory, and power, be unto him that sitteth upon the throne, and unto the Lamb for ever and ever.
> And the four beasts said, Amen. And the four and twenty elders fell down and worshipped him that liveth for ever and ever (Rev. 5:9-14).

The tears, the suffering of this earth will be wiped away by His own loving hand. How wonderful is His glorious promise, "Behold, I make all things new." We shall reign with Christ through the Millennium in our resurrection body. Then the earth and the heavens will be renovated and the new earth and the new heavens will be our final abode.

The wicked also are to be given resurrection bodies (John 5:28,29). Paul tells us in Acts 24:15: "There shall be a resurrection of the dead, both of the just and unjust." The bodies of the dead in Christ will be raised at His coming, but the rest of the dead are not raised until the thousand years are finished (Rev. 20:5). The departed wicked and unbelieving, as long as they are in Hades, continue in their disembodied state, but at the last trump, when the end time shall come and eternity shall begin, they too shall be given resurrection bodies. Those bodies will be the fit habitation for the unholy soul that must dwell in them forever. In the resurrection the unbelieving man will reap all the consummated harvest of his wicked, unrepentant, uncleansed life; for then it is said, "And I saw the dead, small and great, stand before God . . . And whosoever was not found written in the book of life was cast into the lake of fire" (Rev. 20:12 and 15).

I am often asked, "Do you believe in a literal fire?" The best answer I have is this: anything that is a symbol of something is always *less than the reality*. Instead of saying that it is literal, the Holy Spirit is saying that it is even worse. Along those desolate shores the wailing cry of the lost shall echo "unto the ages of the ages." This is the "second death" and this is hell.

No one is in hell at the present time. No one has ever yet gone to hell. The resurrection precedes the final judgment. No one will be in hell until he has stood in judgment before Christ at the Great White Throne and has had the opportunity to answer why he rejected and refused God's grace, mercy, and love. The wicked are all in Hades and there they will remain until the present world ends. Then death and Hades, with all the wicked within it, together with Satan, shall be cast into the depths of perdition to come forth no more forever (Rev. 20). Our Lord said, "Enter ye in at the strait gate: for wide is the gate, and broad is the way, that leadeth to destruction, and many there be which go in thereat" (Matt. 7:13).

An astute scholar once said:

I have read practically all the great works that agnosticism and unbelief have given to the world. I have studied the attacks which have been made against the Christian religion by some of the minds the world has been pleased to call brilliant; and I would be an infidel today were it not for the inescapable fact that I am a man, and I am going somewhere. I am twenty-four hours nearer that somewhere tonight than I was yesternight. I have read all that infidelity has to say. It does not shed one solitary ray of light on the darkness into which I am going. It shall not take away the only guide I have—the Bible—and leave me stone blind.

chapter seven

THE TRAGEDY OF A LOST WORLD

"And to you who are troubled rest with us, when the Lord Jesus shall be revealed from heaven with his mighty angels,

"In flaming fire taking vengeance on them that know not God, and that obey not the gospel of our Lord Jesus Christ:

"Who shall be punished with everlasting destruction from the presence of the Lord, and from the glory of his power" (II Thess. 1:7-9).

"And these shall go away into everlasting (aionius) punishment: but the righteous into life eternal (aionius)" (Matt. 25:46). (Notice that the word used to describe the punishment of the wicked and the state of the righteous is the same word in the Greek.)

"The Lord is not slack concerning his promise, as some men count slackness; but is longsuffering to us-ward, not willing that any should perish, but that all should come to repentance.

"But the day of the Lord will come as a thief in the night; in the which the heavens shall pass away with a great noise, and the elements shall melt with fervent heat, the earth also and the works that are therein shall be burned up" (II Peter 3:9,10).

The Word of God testifies on almost every page that men and women who reject Jesus Christ die and go to a place of waste and loss, to spend their eternity in spiritual darkness.

The strategy and masterpiece of the adversary, the dark prince who rules this world in subterfuge, has been to make men deny his existence and that there is this lost world the Bible calls hell.

There is not a cult that believes in hell. These who proclaim the prissy, pious platitudes of a bloodless, arctic theology, who mutilate and delete from the Word of God anything that would in any way disturb or displease — these are they who reject the teaching of the Holy Book on the truth of perdition and the fact of sin's ultimate and terrible consequence.

The Bible clearly teaches that those who die rejecting Jesus Christ are irremediably and eternally lost. We might wish it were not so; but a careful depth study of divine revelation assures us that God is more concerned that men know about this doctrine — the destiny of lost souls — than perhaps any other. The question of human destiny holds the center of divine revelation.

Men's opinions do not mean anything when they are in opposition to the declaration of God. The Holy Book may be inconsistent with what we feel emotionally and there are many things that may offend our aesthetic tastes. Nevertheless, they are true. The thought of the gas chamber, the electric chair, and the hangman's noose is repulsive. The memory of a missile of death falling upon an innocent population, blotting out a hundred thousand lives in one terrible split second of holocaust, leaving 200,000 victims dying lingering, torturous deaths in the ensuing year, is shocking.

It is fearful to think of the awful carnage left in the wake of battle. The thought of mangled bodies exposed before the morning sun is sickening. Man's inhumanity to man is sometimes unbelievable. The twisted forms of little children in hospitals is a pitiful sight. It is to be feared many of us have so calloused ourselves against the sufferings of our world that few tragedies bother us — only those that hurt us personally. The sin that has eaten its way into the souls of men and warped their purpose, broken them away from God and made them slaves to that which damns, is despicable; but all these things are realities.

Some ask, "Do you have to talk about hell?" Moody used to say that one should never preach on hell unless he preaches in tears. It is true that those who do not preach this truth, who disregard what God has to say about the ultimate end of sin, who fail to tell men what is going to happen because of their repeated refusal of the proffer of Christ's grace, mercy and love, but who preach universalism and restoration, are soon shorn of their power for God. The fires of compassion die out on the altar of their hearts. For them the Word of God increasingly loses its penetrating and piercing power, and soon it is no longer quick and powerful and sharper than a two-edged sword.

Basically there are four classes of people who object to the truth in the Scripture about the lost world:

(1) Those who never give it careful consideration, who, like a parrot, thoughtlessly reproduce the infidel's harangue.

(2) Those who live wicked, licentious, evil lives, who seek to miss that world by denying its existence. All the while they are actually living in the beginning of it and will spend their eternity even as they have spent their lives, in the fulfillment of it.

(3) Those who say that the doctrine and descriptions of hell are too highly figurative. Jesus used the word "Gehenna," the dump outside the city of Jerusalem in the Valley of Hinnom, where all the refuse, garbage and waste of the city was burned. The burning was ceaseless. The smoke rose constantly. Its stench, when the wind blew across the city, was unbearable. When Jesus used the word "Gehenna," the picture in people's minds was a vivid one, and many who listened to Him trembled as they thought of the comparison.

When we say that a figure is a symbol we do not in any way minimize what it represents, for the symbol is always less reality than the object itself. For example, we gather about the communion table to partake of the elements of bread and wine that speak to us of the contorted, twisting form of our Saviour on the scaffold of Calvary — His dripping blood, His broken body — but they are only symbols that testify to something that none of us can ever fully conceive of or appreciate. If we say that the terminology of the New Testament is expressed in figures of speech, we do not minimize the lesson on the reality of hell. The reality was so difficult to express that Jesus used the strongest language that could be found. Hell is more terrible than even the similes and the figures that are used to describe it.

(4) Some say that God is too merciful to send a soul to hell. There is much misunderstanding at this point. Nowhere does the Bible say that God ever sentenced a soul to hell. The infinite, eternal, inexhaustible love of God never decreed that a soul should spend eternity in hell. "For God sent not his Son into the world to condemn the world; but that the world through him might be saved" (John 3:17). Suicide is not murder! In the case of a murder, someone else is responsible for the victim's death; in a suicide the one who takes the life and the one who dies is one and the same. When a man rejects Jesus Christ, he commits spiritual suicide. In this case the condemnation and death is alone the responsibility of the Christ-rejector. God is not in any way responsible. No soul ever goes out into the dark night of eternity without Christ unless it goes over and past every possible barrier that the love of God can place between it and the lost world. Men go to hell because that is where they choose to go. It is the world of their choice. Men do not want to come to God on God's conditions, on God's terms. They deliberately refuse and reject Jesus Christ, and in so doing they accept the consequences of their choice. Our Lord loves those who reject His redemption. He loves

the souls of those who die without Him, who go out beyond the reach of His saving hand. He never ceases to love them.

Have you ever tried to help somebody that would not let you help him? Have you ever sensed the futility, the frustration of it? Hear it in the words of Jesus when He said, "Ye will not come to me, that ye might have life" (John 5:40). Similarly and infinitely magnified is the love of Christ toward the lost. If you will not have Him, if you refuse Him, if you say, as the mob said on that awful day He was impaled upon the scaffold, "We will not have this man to reign over us," then, with His eyes filled with tears and His heart broken in the pain of unrequited love, He will allow you to go into a world where you will never have to see His face, never have to live in the guilt of His rejected love forever.

The love of God permits the lost soul that does not want Him to spend eternity even as he has spent life — without Him. If you pillow your head in the last sleep without the Saviour, it will not be because He does not love you. It will not be because He did not tenderly plead with you through the delicate ministry of the Holy Spirit. It will not be because His Gospel was not pressed by His faithful messengers against your heart. It will not be because you were not stirred, moved and challenged. It will not be because the testimony of the Word of God was not clear and plain; it will be, in the light of divine revelation, because you deliberately chose the dark. God lets you choose. Jesus said, "And this is the condemnation, that light is come into the world, and men loved darkness rather than light, because their deeds were evil" (John 3:19). Notice, they *love* darkness, they *prefer* darkness. It is *their choice!*

Why do I believe there is a hell? Because common sense teaches it and justice insists upon it. Science says every deed has its inevitable consequence. When we sin, suffering follows as certain as day follows night. Every textbook on physiology and psychology verifies this truth. The drunkard eats the fruit of his own devices. The young libertine must expect a blighted old age. There is many a tombstone that tells of a body rotted by abuse and sin. The nation that hurls the world into the yawning abyss of war pays with her own dismemberment and division. The beaten corpse of the cringing Mussolini, exposed and grotesque in the square of Milan, proves that sin pays its inevitable wages. Sin damns as sure as water drowns and fire burns. The inexorable laws of nature thunder more loudly than the Bible, that "Whatsoever a man soweth, that shall he also reap" (Gal. 6:7).

Men can sneer at God, they can procrastinate the love of Christ, postpone life's most important decision, but they are sentencing themselves by each refusal to an existence — and eternal night — without God. You can sneer at His work, disregard the fact of judgment, but all the time the sin you are committing gathers momentum like a threatening storm; and one day it will strike you with lightning-like revenge. Such is the culminating and accumulating power of the sin of disobedience.

The laws of society are expressions of our belief in the wisdom of the Bible doctrine of hell. We have cemeteries because it is necessary to separate the living from the dead, or else we will all die. It is imperative, in the interest of humanity, to separate the sane from the insane, the innocent from the guilty. These measures are absolutely essential to maintain some kind of order in society, and thus preserve humanity.

There must be two worlds ahead. A world where those go who want the fellowship of God, who willingly, gladly meet the conditions of God as defined in His Holy Word, who accept the grace of God as revealed in the finished work of Jesus Christ, man's only Redeemer and Saviour, who desire the benediction of the Holy Spirit's presence in their lives and the new life offered by forgiveness and regeneration, and who want to spend their endless eternity in the presence of this wonderful One, the Lord Jesus Christ.

On the contrary, there must be a world where men go who do not want these values and relationships and who, in overt disobedience, refuse the Word of God, the Son of God, who make a mock of the Spirit of grace and the pleadings of the Holy Spirit, the miracle of regeneration and the offer of divine forgiveness for sin. It can be said reverently, God owes it to the righteous, to those who fling themselves upon Christ and claim Him as their Lord and Saviour, to free them one day not only from the power of sin but from the very presence of sin forever.

There are people you don't invite to your home because they are unfit associates for your loved ones. For God to allow the unregenerate, vile, unholy, uncleansed, murderer, adulterer, liar, reprobate, Christ-rejector to live eternally in the society of those who have accepted the redemption of Jesus Christ, would re-create the basic problem that alienated man in the first place. For those

115

who have been made new creatures, who have claimed a faith that transformed them, to have to dwell with those without this experience would bring not only incompatibility but would also turn heaven into hell. As long as God regards His sovereignty, His holiness and the sacrifice of His Son on Calvary's cross, there must be a world where men go who do not want and will not have Jesus Christ. I know people who do not want the church, let alone Christ, who do not want to be with Christians, let alone with Christ.

Some years ago a friend invited me to play golf with him and two friends of his. When we met to play, he introduced me as Dr. MacArthur, a minister. One of the foursome said, "If you're a minister, I don't want to play with you. I don't want to have a thing to do with you."

I said, "Well, if you don't want to, that's all right."

He replied, "You'd ruin my game. If you went along, I'd have to watch my language; and the first thing you know I'd be in such a knot that I couldn't even hit the ball. There isn't anything that makes me more miserable than having a minister around."

My friend was embarrassed. He offered to separate and play with me, but I did not want to break up their game so I found someone else to play with.

You can readily see the analogy. I am merely a representative of Christ, but this man didn't want me around. Should you force that man to go to heaven? Can you imagine anyone who would be more miserable? This gives an idea of what heaven and hell are like. Something has to happen to you before heaven will ever be heaven. Otherwise the only place that is left is hell.

There is nothing mysterious about hell. It is where people go who do not want Jesus Christ. The decision made here is finalized at the moment of death and there is no second chance. The Bible says: "He which is filthy let him be filthy still: and he that is righteous, let him be righteous still" (Rev. 22:11).

There is a recompense of reward. Domitian, Trajan, and millions like them, suffered little in this world, though they fed Christians as meat to the lions, as dry wood to the flames, subjecting them to all the human hell their perverted minds could possibly dream. The Word of God says of them: "To whom is reserved the blackness of darkness forever" (Jude 13).

Will there be a difference in the degree of suffering? Of course! God's justice is perfect. The direction our lives assume is the important thing. When men fulfill their lives in a movement that is away from God and deviate from His will, the tendency is to accelerate the pace. When men move toward God, and toward the fulfillment of His will, the tendency is the same — only one is going away from God; the other is drawing closer to Him.

Do not refuse the glorious Saviour who died over 1900 years ago on Golgotha's Hill; because the dark world, where dwell the souls who do not want Him, is indeed so dark that it beggars human language to bring before our thoughts, minds, and hearts the grim realities of its tragedy.

There is a soft, supersentimentalism that deprecates and denounces the preaching of hell. But Jesus said if your eye or your hand has anything to do with your sin, you had better gouge out your eye, you had better chop off your hand, rather than be cast into the fire of hell (Matt. 18:8). Whatever the sin is, however small, that keeps you from Christ, that is the sin that binds and chains you to eternal darkness. Without Christ there is no light, only darkness forever. "I am the light of the world; he that followeth me shall not walk in darkness, but shall have the light of life" (John 8:12). The simplest definition of hell is the absence of Jesus Christ. Without Christ, who is the light, there is nothing left but darkness.

We know there is a hell because of the testimony of those who have gone there. Only one time is the curtain drawn back, allowing a glimpse of the world of the lost.

"And it came to pass, that the beggar died, and was carried by the angels into Abraham's bosom: the rich man also died, and was buried;

"And in hell he lifted up his eyes, being in torments, and seeth Abraham afar off, and Lazarus in his bosom.

"And he cried and said, Father Abraham, have mercy on me, and send Lazarus, that he may dip the tip of his finger in water, and cool my tongue; for I am tormented in this flame" (Luke 16:22-24).

In spite of the historical and allegorical interpretation of this Scripture, and with the consciousness of the various shades of meaning that have been put upon it, it nevertheless teaches two things that cannot be refuted or altered:

(1) The rich man was without God, and suffering acutely.

(2) Lazarus, comforted by Abraham, was obviously conscious of the presence of God.

Strangely enough, there is no evidence that the rich man wanted to change his state — at least he did not ask to change it, or else he knew that change was impossible. He had made a choice for eternity. However, he did want to warn others not to make the same wrong decision he had made. Similarly, for example, alcoholics will not give up the bottle, but they plead with others not to become victims of drink.

Edward Gibbon, author of *The Decline and Fall of the Roman Empire,* was rated as one of the strongest infidels of his day. When he died in London, his last words were, "All is lost, irrevocably lost; all is dark and doubtful." He realized too late that his choice, made all through life, was at last crystallized in permanency.

When Voltaire felt the final stroke that terminated in death, he was overcome with remorse. Infidels rushed to his side to prevent him from making a statement that would reflect upon his standing as the leading infidel of his day. He cursed them to their faces, drove them from his presence and said, "Begone; it is you that brought me to my present condition. Leave me, I say — begone — what a wretched glory this is you have produced for me." Then, in hostility toward God and man, he turned his face toward the wall and cried, "I must die, abandoned of God and man!"

Robert Ley, the Nazi propagandist and inventor of the Rosenberg theology, repudiated his anti-Semitism, his anti-Christian views while waiting trial in the Nuremberg prison. Echoing the words of Voltaire, he wrote, "Tonight I die, abandoned of God," then hanged himself in his cell. The dying confession of leading unbelievers is that in life they declared: "No God, no Christ, no Bible, no hell, no heaven — it is all fable and myth." But in death, as life's stream trickled to its finishing drop, almost without exception where we have the record of their words, these men became as orthodox as Puritan preachers and died in the consciousness of the fact that they had chosen an eternity of despair and were dying without hope and without Christ. Why, when they knew that, didn't they accept Him? Because even in death they did not want Him.

In the 264 chapters of the New Testament God reminds us 234 times of the reality of this hopeless world, nearly one verse for every chapter in the New Testament. If life's road were 264 miles long and you saw 234 signboards that warned: "This road leads away from God into the dark night of hell"; and if you did not turn around and go the other way, you could never place the blame on the one who put the signs on the highway. God has put signs on the highway all through the New Testament, and if you are lost, you can blame only yourself, for it is your disposition, your desire, your chosen direction that has caused the wretchedness of your soul.

The Bible says more about hell than it does about heaven. If there is no such place then the Bible is unreliable. If the Bible is unreliable, then Jesus Christ is not the Son of God; if He is not the Son of God, then you are without hope, with no anchor for your soul, waiting for the light to flicker out and plunge you into the darkness of oblivion. God says there is this world, and it is because of it that He gave His only begotten Son, that whosoever believeth on Him should *not* perish.

Scripture warns us about this world. "Then shall he say also unto them on the left hand, Depart from me, ye cursed, into everlasting fire, prepared for the devil and his angels: And these shall go away into everlasting punishment: but the righteous into life eternal" (Matt. 25:41 & 46).

"And to you who are troubled rest with us, when the Lord Jesus shall be revealed from heaven with his mighty angels,

"In flaming fire taking vengeance on them that know not God, and that obey not the Gospel of our Lord Jesus Christ:

"Who shall be punished with everlasting destruction from the presence of the Lord, and from the glory of His power" (II Thess. 1:7-9). No one can misunderstand these words; they mean what they say. John tells us about the judgment of the Christ-rejectors: "And whosoever was not found written in the book of life was cast into the lake of fire" (Rev. 20:15).

The lost world is more of a certainty than that you or I will be alive tomorrow. It is no guess; it is an authoritative declaration. Jesus said there are two gates. There is no way you can change it.

"Enter ye in at the strait gate: for wide is the gate, and broad is the way, that leadeth to destruction, and many there be which go in thereat: Because strait is the gate, and narrow is the way, which leadeth unto life, and few there be that find it" (Matt. 7:13, 14).

Jesus taught there are two ways of living. He said that men could follow him or the dictates of their own depraved hearts; that they could go His way or their way;

that they could listen either to Him or to Satan. Jesus further said there are only two destinies and all of us are fulfilling ourselves in one or the other. Your life is moving second by second toward heaven or hell. Direc tion plus time equals your final destiny.

He said, "And these shall go away into everlasting (aionios) punishment: but the righteous into life eternal" (aionios) (Matt. 25:46). The word "aionios" occurs seventy times in the New Testament. The word that is applied to the punishment of unbelievers is also applied to the life possessed by believers; to the salvation in which they rejoice (Heb. 9:12); to the glory to which they look forward (II Cor. 4:17); to those mansions in which they hope to dwell (II Cor. 5:1); and to the inheritance which they expect to enjoy (Heb. 9:15). If, therefore, the word "everlasting" does not mean everlasting when applied to the wicked and unbelieving, then what security do we have that it means everlasting when applied to the life of blessedness and glory of the redeemed? What warrant has anyone to single out seven instances from the seventy and say in these seven instances that the word does not mean everlasting? The Scripture says those who die *without* Jesus Christ spend their eternity forever without Him and that those who die *in* Jesus Christ spend their eternity with Him.

There is a lost world because of the sacrifice of God, in the death of our Lord Jesus Christ on the cross. Unless there is a hell to save the sinner from, then the crucifixion of Jesus was God's colossal blunder. Christ died that "we might not perish." "For as in Adam all die" because of sin, so now "in Christ shall all be made alive." As the

122

federal head of the new race, He broke the power that had already broken all men; and as the victor He offers to you and to me His triumph, His very life, but solely and only on the basis of regeneration.

My wonderful Dad used to tell about a man who rode home with him after my Dad had preached a funeral service. The man commented, "I enjoyed your sermon. More preachers ought to preach on the love of God. If there's anything I hate it's these preachers who preach about hell all the time."

My father replied, "Is there any particular verse in the Bible that you like best?" realizing there was probably only one verse he could quote.

"Oh, yes, the one that says 'God loved the world.'"

Dad then helped him along in quoting John 3:16, "For God so loved the world, that He gave His only begotten son." Dad stopped him there and asked, "Now isn't it wonderful that God loved the world so much He would give Himself in the person of His own son as man's Saviour? Isn't that wonderful? — *that's* love."

They went on into the verse, 'that whosoever believeth in Him should not perish." Again, Dad asked, "Now what does that mean? Why did God give His son?"

The man replied, "Well, so that we might not perish."

Closing in, my father continued, "What does it mean to perish?"

The man thought a moment and answered, "I guess that means to go to hell, doesn't it?"

Then Dad said, "That is exactly what it says — God gave His only begotten son that whosoever believeth in Him should not perish but have everlasting life." And my father led that man to Jesus Christ that day.

God would never have permitted His beloved Son to be crushed by hell's awful power; God would never have allowed the Morning Star to fall from its orbit; God would never have allowed His Anointed to be trampled by the vulgar feet of those who blasphemed His name; He would never have permitted the death of His Only Begotten, *unless His holy and eternal purpose was the redemption of your soul and mine.* So the Scripture says, "Who gave himself a ransom for all" (I Tim. 2:6). "Christ also hath once suffered for sins, the just for the unjust, that he might bring us to God . . . " (I Peter 3:18).

This regal Christ, with one hand reaches into your life and mine, and with the other reaches into the dazzling brilliance of the pure holiness of God's presence. Through the efficacy of the forgiveness that He made possible by His own shed blood, by taking the penalty of your sin and mine, we, by His death, are justified and are given access into the very presence of God. If there is no hell to save us from, then there was no need for Jesus Christ to invade our world, become part of us and go the way of the cross to die for our sins. Hell is real, or else Christ's death on Calvary was the greatest price ever paid for folly. Someone has rightfully asked, "Should God have consented to let His Son leave heaven and come into this cruel world, suffer persecution, and be nailed to a cross to die, if there is no hell to save people from?"

The late Dr. Clarence McCartney said, "If there is no hell, no future, no eternal punishment upon sin, then Christianity is a costly and tremendous remedy, but an unnecessary one, for man did not require it, and will be saved without it."

What is hell like? I have seen some people in the beginning of it and so have you. Have you ever seen a dope addict at the end? All of the metaphors, all the similes, all of the adjectives, all of the words that the Koine Greek possessed, Jesus used, to tell about it and I believe there was always a sob in His throat. He said it was a world of utter darkness and one of eternal separation. How terrible to be in eternity in a black existence without Christ!

Jesus said concerning Judas: "It had been good for that man if he had not been born" (Matt. 26:24). He was saying that if Judas could have been annihilated, or could have gone out of existence, it would be good. But because he was born, he will live forever in perdition.

How long will hell last? The longer a man goes on in sin the deeper down he goes. Sin realizes itself in more sin. If you will not repent in this life, what evidence is there that you will in the aeons of eternity? Logic says you will go farther and farther away. What you are you will become increasingly. Repentance becomes impossible after willful sinning passes a certain point. God permits you to live the life you want to live.

Hell is a place where there is no hope. A sick, disabled individual has hope of some day being well and strong. If one has a debt hanging over him, he has hope that some day it will be paid. The business man who can barely pay expenses is hopeful for a better day. Whatever may be our lot here, we have hope for the future. In hell there is no hope. There is not even the hope of annihilation. Charles Spurgeon said, "On every chain is written, 'forever.' Up above their heads they read, 'forever.' Their eyes are galled, their hearts are pained with the thought that it is forever. Oh, if I could tell you that hell would one day be burned out and that those who were lost might be saved, there would be a jubilee in hell at the very thought of it. But it cannot be — it is 'forever' they are cast into outer darkness."

God has done all He can to prevent men from entering the lost world. If the love of Christ will not humble a man and draw him to the saving power of the wonderful Christ, then certainly no other force will ever do it. If a man pushes aside the pleading Christ, certainly the environment where souls live without the influence of the Holy Spirit will never be conducive to anything that would ever cause repentance. That is why the Word of God urges, "Now is the accepted time, now is the day of salvation" (II Cor. 6:2). Do not stay away another hour from Jesus Christ. Let Him forgive you. Let Him into your life. Spend today and tomorrow and all the rest of the days of your life in His companionship and anticipate the unspeakable glory of an eternity with Him — free from sin and death forever. Certainly one reason for never wanting to spend eternity in the loneliness of the lost world is because Satan will be there. "And the devil that deceived them was cast into the lake of fire and brimstone, where the beast and false prophet are, and shall be tormented day and night forever and ever" (Rev. 20:10).

There will be no love there. "But the children of the kingdom shall be cast out into outer darkness: there shall be weeping and gnashing of teeth" (Matt. 8:12). This indicates that there will be selfish remorse and bitter regret.

There will be no singing there. What a contrast is the picture portrayed for us in the great scene of the revelator:

> And they sung a new song, saying, Thou art worthy to take the book and to open the seals thereof: for thou wast slain, and hast redeemed us to God by thy blood out of every kindred, and tongue, and people, and nation; And hast made us unto our God kings and priests: and we shall reign on the earth. And I beheld, and I heard the voice of many angels round about the throne and the beasts and the elders: and the number of them was ten thousand times ten thousand, and thousands of thousands; Saying with a loud voice, Worthy is the Lamb that was slain to receive power, and riches, and wisdom, and strength, and honour, and glory, and blessing (Rev. 5:9-12).

I do not want to go to hell because of hell's vile companionship. "But the fearful, (those who hold back from following Christ) and unbelieving, (Christ-rejectors) and the abominable, and murderers, and whoremongers, and sorcerers, and idolaters, and all liars, shall have their part in the lake which burneth with fire and brimstone: which is the second death" (Rev. 21:8).

I do not want to go to hell because of unending memory. The only message that ever came from heaven to the rich man in hell was a message of two words: "Son, *remember*." Scripture says that hell is a place where "their worm dieth not." Memories will still linger. They will make hell a place of unrelieved remorse.

I do not want to go to hell because Jesus will not be there. Jesus Christ stands between every man and hell. Jesus is the way; He opened the highway for lost sinners. "He hath made him to be sin for us . . . that we might

127

be made the righteousness of God in Him" (II Cor. 5:21). "Who his own self bare our sins in his own body on the tree, that we, being dead to sins, should live unto righteousness: by whose stripes ye were healed" (I Peter 2:24). You need not go to this awful hell. Ample, adequate provision has been made for your deliverance; but if you fight against the revelation of God, ignore His word, refuse His will, disregard the pleadings of the Holy Spirit, reject Jesus Christ as your Lord and Saviour, follow the ways of sin and live in unbelief, you can never charge God with the responsibility of sentencing you to hell. God is doing all an infinite God can do through a thousand agencies of His grace to keep you out of hell. If you find yourself there, you and you alone are to blame. Jesus said, "I am the way, the truth, and the life; no man cometh unto the Father, but by me" (John 14:6). He said, "I am the door: by me if any man enter in, he shall be saved . . . " (John 10:9). Christ is the one door of hope in the valley of Achar, the only healing balm in Gilead. "Neither is there salvation in any other: for there is none other name under heaven given among men, whereby we must be saved" (Acts 4:12). Change the direction of your life and live for Him.

D. L. Moody tells of a father whose son had broken his mother's heart and sent her to a premature grave. The father hoped the death of the mother would cause the son to give up the kind of life he was living, but soon after her death he went deeper into sin. One night, as he was leaving the home for another orgy of dissipation, his father asked him if he would spend the evening with him because he was anxious to talk with him about the future. The young man refused him.

The father further pleaded and then said, "Son, you broke your mother's heart; and if you are determined to break my heart because of the sordid way you are living, I'm not going to let you go out without making one more desperate effort to save you." Then, standing in the doorway, he said, "If you leave this house, Son, you must go over this body of mine."

The ungrateful son drew back his fist and sent it crashing against his father's jaw, leaped over his prostrate body, and went out into his night of sin, shame and ruin. You say that was a terrible thing to do, what a violation of love. But did you ever stop to think that God gave His son, put Him in your path, and that now He stands before you with blood on His brow, nail prints in His hands, pleading for you to accept Him, pleading for you not to go past Him into the night of hopeless despair? What a thought it is that there is not a single soul who will go to hell without going over the murdered body of God's Son! You must trample the blood of Jesus Christ under your feet to be lost. "Of how much sorer punishment, suppose ye, shall he be thought worthy, who hath trodden under foot the Son of God . . . ?" (Heb. 10:29). Hear Him as He says, "Him that cometh to me I will in no wise cast out" (John 6:37).

"Except ye repent, ye shall all likewise perish" (Luke 13:5). " . . . Believe on the Lord Jesus Christ, and thou shalt be saved, and thy house" (Acts 16:31). If you reject Him again, you set your sail toward the blackness of an eternal night without God.

The story is told of a coal miner who lost his lamp

in the darkness. No one knew how long he searched for the light but finally, weak from exhaustion, hunger, and thirst, he fell and death came to his release and relief. Strangely enough, when they found him, his hand was just inches from the light.

I wonder how many souls go out into the darkness of eternity who, not once but many times, have been consciously only inches from the light and refused it. It must be said of them that they chose darkness rather than light. What act could be more insane than to walk out into the eternal night with no God, with no hope?

Christ is the light. No man, by any decree of God, needs to go to hell. "The Lord is not slack concerning His promise, as some men count slackness; but is longsuffering to us-ward, not willing that any should perish, but that all should come to repentance" (II Peter 3:9). The Word of God says that Jesus Christ has provided a way of escape for every man, that He has "not come to call the righteous, but sinners to repentance" (Matt. 9:13). He wants you. What do *you* want?

We are assured that "He that believeth on the Son hath everlasting life; and he that believeth not the Son shall not see life, but the wrath of God abideth on him" (John 3:36). (Note the present tense; the wrath of God *is* abiding on him.) The rejection of His love brings with it condemnation. It is automatic. To live without it, to refuse Jesus Christ means to live and die without Him *and that is Hell.*

chapter eight

HEAVEN IS A REALITY

"After this I beheld, and lo a great multitude, which no man could number, of all nations, and kindreds, and people, and tongues, stood before the throne, and before the Lamb, clothed with white robes, and palms in their hands;

"And cried with a loud voice, saying, Salvation to our God which sitteth upon the throne, and unto the Lamb.

"And all the angels stood round about the throne, and about the elders and the four beasts, and fell before the throne on their faces, and worshipped God,

"Saying, Amen: Blessing, and glory, and wisdom, and thanksgiving, and honour, and power, and might, be unto our God for ever and ever. Amen.

"And one of the elders answered, saying unto me, What are these which are arrayed in white robes? and whence came they?

"And I said unto him, Sir, thou knowest. And he said to me, These are they which came out of great tribulation, and have washed their robes, and made them white in the blood of the Lamb.

"Therefore are they before the throne of God, and

serve him day and night in his temple: and he that sitteth on the throne shall dwell among them.

"They shall hunger no more, neither thirst any more; neither shall the sun light on them, nor any heat.

"For the Lamb which is in the midst of the throne shall feed them, and shall lead them unto living fountains of waters: and God shall wipe away all tears from their eyes" (Rev. 7:9-17).

"And I saw a new heaven and a new earth: for the first heaven and the first earth were passed away; and there was no more sea.

"And I John saw the holy city, new Jerusalem, coming down from God out of heaven, prepared as a bride adorned for her husband.

"And I heard a great voice out of heaven saying, Behold, the tabernacle of God is with men, and he will dwell with them, and they shall be his people, and God Himself shall be with them, and be their God.

"And God shall wipe away all tears from their eyes; and there shall be no more death, neither sorrow, nor crying, neither shall there be anymore pain: for the former things are passed away" (Rev. 21:1-4).

"And he shewed me a pure river of water of life, clear as crystal, proceeding out of the throne of God and of the Lamb.

"In the midst of the street of it, and on either side of the river, was there the tree of life, which bare twelve manner of fruits, and yielded her fruit every month: and the leaves of the tree were for the healing of the nations.

"And there shall be no more curse: but the throne of God and of the Lamb shall be in it; and his servants shall serve him:

"And they shall see his face; and his name shall be in their foreheads.

"And there shall be no night there; and they need no candle, neither light of the sun; for the Lord God giveth them light: and they shall reign for ever and ever.

"And he said unto me, These sayings are faithful and true: and the Lord God of the holy prophets sent his angel to shew unto his servants the things which must shortly be done.

"Behold, I come quickly: blessed is he that keepeth the sayings of the prophecy of this book" (Rev. 22:1-7).

"Let not your heart be troubled: ye believe in God, believe also in me. In my Father's house are many mansions: if it were not so, I would have told you. I go to prepare a place for you, And if I go and prepare a place for you, I will come again, and receive you unto myself; that where I am, there ye may be also" (John 14:1-3).

We are definitely tied to the world of our experience, and we can never learn anything new unless we can associate it with something we already know. When we talk about the celestial world, it is very difficult to find any similes of comparison with which to attach and associate the realities of the world that is to come. Even the most beautiful music ever wafted on the air, the most glorious sunset in the sky or the sea cannot express even in a measure the magnificence and beauties of the wonders of that world called heaven. It is completely beyond human comprehension. As the Scripture says, "Eye hath not seen, nor ear heard, neither have entered into the heart of man, the things which God hath prepared for them that love him" (I Cor. 2:9). The Scripture goes on to say that our only possible discernment of these things is under the inspiration, direction and revelation of the Holy Spirit. "But God hath revealed them unto us by his Spirit . . . " (I Cor. 2:10).

Heaven is a prepared place for a prepared people. It is one of the most meaningful rewards God holds out to those who accept His Son as Saviour and who, in yielding their lives to Him, show forth their title to eternal fellowship with the redeemed host of glory. It is a noble, inspiring, cheering doctrine. It has encouraged the martyr as he sacrificed his life for Christ at the stake, and sustained the bed-ridden Christian through long suffering. This thrilling prospect gives us fortitude to bear the trials, temptations, loneliness and sufferings of life with an unbowed head and unfaltering step. However, there is not one among us who has not at sometime in his life experienced the doubt that brings him face to face with the desire to be certain of the existence of that celestial world.

We have already talked about the fact that emotion says there is a heaven. As we have seen, it is an instinct, a capacity of the human soul. Even without the knowledge gained from the Bible it would still remain an undeniable expectation in the hearts of men everywhere.

That which is universally persistent in the nature of man must be natural; and if the belief in immortality be natural to man, it rises out of this intuitive nature and will find its realization. The wild geese go northward in the spring because a strange longing overpowers them; and then as autumn approaches they wing their way southward across the trackless land and sea to the place they intuitively know to be home. How magnificent that instinct! Man is a creature of reason and intelligence; nevertheless, he is also a creature of instinct. There is an instinctive longing for life after death, and because instincts are prophecies, there is the reality to satisfy this yearning. That reality begins a vital, living, relationship with the eternal Christ. He imparts a quality of life that makes immortality heaven instead of hell. In every Christian's heart there is a longing for unbroken communion with the Saviour. That desire was placed in man by God and it grows with the passing of the years.

Fairness says there is a heaven — justice demands it. Decency, righteousness, honor and honesty demand it. The world is cursed with inequity and sorrow. God began it right in the first place; but man, through his failing, turned order into chaos. Through man's rebellion death invaded the world. We live in a moral world but man is immoral. There is a day coming when perfect justice will be meted out by a sovereign God.

Is it justice that Nero and Diocletian should throw Christians to the lions, wade in innocent blood and never be accountable for their crimes? Shall the Son of God be impaled on the cross and never be exalted? Justice unmistakably tells us there is a heaven for those who have accepted Christ as their Lord and Saviour and love Him with all their hearts, where they will dwell with Him forever. Justice also cries out there is a hell — a world of loss and darkness—where the indifferent, careless, Christ-rejector will spend eternity. If you are not related to Jesus Christ by the miracle of faith, if you do not know Him as your personal Saviour, if you have not accepted

Him, then the Scripture says eternity will be even as your life has been. It will be spent out of His presence forever, in a world of emptiness, waste and loss.

There is another life beyond the brief years of this life. A choice of destinies awaits the soul of man, a life now and forever with Christ, or a life now and forever without Christ. Eternity only makes your present relationship permanent. Your eternal existence is a fact, but you decide, by what you do with Christ, whether you will spend your eternity in the light or in the night.

Faith says there is a heaven. Faith is confidence in the Word of God, and it inerrantly teaches there is a heaven. Doubt it and the whole Christian system would be destroyed.

The only authority on spiritual matters is the Word of God — the Bible.

Some great men of science are discovering evidence for the existence of the soul and the inference of immortality apart from divine revelation. Dr. Gustav Stromberg tells us how an electrical field enters the lip of the blastopore, supervises the development of the embryo, becomes the kinetic system that governs all of the stimuli and responses of the body and then leaves fully developed and intact at the moment of death.

Dr. H. S. Burr reports: "All living organisms are implanted in electrical fields. These leave in death. These fields are independent of the matter involved and certainly suggest the soul."

As we previously noted, within the cycle of seven years every particle of tissue, fiber and encephalon within the human body is replaced, even the very tissue of the brain.

136

Yet the perpendicular "I" within the body never changes. But even all this is only inference.

We who know Christ have a faith that clarions to the world the fact of His heaven, faith founded on the Word of God. Faith assures the Christian that he has a city "whose builder and maker is God." Heaven is a reality!

Heaven is a place. Jesus said, "I go to prepare a place for you." The word "place" in the Greek means a "home." Some say heaven is a state, a condition; but it is more than that — it is a place, a home. It is not merely state of mind but a city as well, a city that has foundations. The new Jerusalem, as described in the Scripture, will cover an area as large as from the Pacific Coast to Chicago, and from the Canadian border to the Gulf of Mexico. Hebrews 9:24 tells us that Christ has already entered into heaven now to appear in the presence of God for us. He has gone to prepare a place for us. We are not to be disembodied spirits in the world to come, but redeemed spirits, in redeemed bodies, in a redeemed society, in a redeemed universe; and God is the architect.

As someone has said, God is never embarrassed for want of room. When He made the earth, He did not use the moon as His model. We talk about size and immediately we think of the infinite mind of God. Why, this earth is so small it is a wonder God has not forgotten that he ever made it! But with all, I believe it is the theatre of the universe because God made it for man. "The heaven, even the heavens, are the Lord's: but the earth hath he given to the children of men" (Psa. 115:16).

A. K. Morrison, the brilliant scientist, tells us that

conditions for life on this tiny planet, earth, demand billions of minute, involved circumstances that must appear simultaneously in the same, infinitesimal moment. So our relative smallness does not depreciate our significance. There is no other planet that meets these conditions. This is the planet God constituted and stored and then declared, "Let us make man."

Someone said you can bore a hole in the sun and pour into it 1,200,000 earths the size of ours and still have room for 4,300,000 moons to lie around the edge. The diameter of the sun, which is 93 million miles away from us, is 385,000 miles, but is not very big in comparison with our nearest star, Alpha Centauri, which is five times larger than our sun.

The moon is only 211,463 miles away. You could walk to it in 27 years at 24 miles a day. We are going to spend 40 billion dollars to send a man there. At 25,000 miles an hour it will take only eight and one-half hours for him to land. A ray of light travels approximately 186,000 miles per second, so a beam of light would reach the moon in one and one-half seconds. We can't go that fast yet, but if we could we'd reach Mercury in 4½ minutes, 50 million miles away; in 2 minutes 18 seconds, Venus, 26 million miles away; and in 4 minutes 21 seconds, Mars, 34 million miles distant.

Next comes Jupiter, 367 million miles, giant planet of the sky, champion of the starry world, with its four moons and two big belts of shining vapor; but he is only our next-door neighbor. It would take just 35 minutes 11 seconds to reach Jupiter.

In the southwest is Saturn with her rings that had

Galileo guessing. Twice as far away as Jupiter, it would take 1 hour 11 seconds to reach Saturn by light beam. At 25,000 miles per hour it would take 1,241 and two-third days or nearly four years to get there, a distance of about 790 million miles from the earth.

Next comes Uranus, 1,608,800 miles away; and then Neptune, nearly 3 billion miles away. If you counted 100 miles a minute, it would take you 57 years counting day and night to count the miles to Neptune.

And then there is Pluto, 2,668,000,000 miles from the earth. Traveling at 25,000 miles an hour it would take 4,446 and two-third days to reach the planet Pluto — more than 12 years. But we aren't out very far yet. We are still in our tiny solar system! Alpha Centauri is ten times farther out, or about 20 billion miles. The North Star is 14 times farther, or about 400 billion miles. But even that isn't far. Light traveling at 186,000 miles per second would take 150 years to reach Betelgeuse, which is 880 quadrillion miles from earth. The diameter of this great star (200,000,000 miles) is greater than that of the earth's orbit!

The whole solar system — sun, moon, earth, and all the other planets, is at this moment flying through space, 400 times faster than a rocket. We are heading straight for the beautiful constellation, Lyra. With every second of the clock's tick we are ten miles nearer, and have blasted about 150 miles through space since you read this sentence. The English astronomer Professor Fred Hoyle advances the intriguing idea that the creation of the starry worlds is still going on out in the vast endlessness of space. Who conceived of all this and brought it into existence? What answer do we have if we do not say God!

Albert Einstein said the universe witnesses to a great cosmic intelligence. We Christians believe the Bible identifies the Cosmic Intelligence. "All things were made by him; and without him was not anything made that was made" (John 1:3). If God could make a universe like this one and eighteen known solar systems beyond ours, with millions more that we do not yet know about, and we are part of it, and God says, "I go to prepare a place for you," *what must it mean?*

Because God loves beauty, heaven will be incomparably beautiful. A description of it is found in Revelation 21 and 22. The God of the Bible is pre-eminently a God of beauty. Ask, as Dr. W. E. Beiderwolf asked, "Who painted the butterfly's wings with all those gorgeous hues? Who threw around the evening sun a drapery of a thousand colors? Who put the red on the robin's breast? From whose palette were the colors mixed that gave the rose its blushing charm and touched the lily with its dreamy white? Who taught the raindrop to take a ray of light from heaven's shining orb and pencil it on the sky in one huge arch of bewildering elegance? God did it all." He made everything beautiful, but sin marred it. The whole creation has fallen in sympathy with fallen man and "groans and travails together in pain until now," but enough is left of the primal beauty to show how God loves beauty. He has told us in His Word, "The creation itself also shall be delivered from the bondage of corruption into the glorious liberty of the children of God" (Rom. 8:21-23). In heaven we will find God's beauty unmarred and at its very best.

A little Swedish girl was walking in the evening with her father, and looking up into the diamond-studded night sky said, "Daddy, if the wrong side of heaven is so beautiful, what must the right side be like?"

John got a glimpse of heaven and tried his best to tell us about it, but he could only use familiar symbols when he said the walls are of jasper, the foundation garnished with precious stones, every gate is a pearl, and the city is of pure gold. That was the best comparison John could make. But even that is utterly inadequate.

A child, congenitally blind, knew of the beauties of the world only from her mother's lips. A noted surgeon performed a series of operations on her eyes with excellent results. As the last bandages dropped away, the little girl ran into her mother's arms, then to the window, then to the open door; and as the majestic beauties of earth rolled into her vision for the first time, she flew back to her mother and said, with eyes shining in wonder, "Oh, Mother, why didn't you tell me it was so beautiful?" Wiping away her tears of joy the mother said, "My precious child, I tried to tell you but I just couldn't do it!"

One of these days when we go sweeping through those gates of pearl and catch our first vision of the enrapturing beauty of that world where Jesus Christ is, I think we will find John and say, "John, why didn't you tell us it was so beautiful?" And John will say, "After I received my vision I tried to tell you when I wrote the twenty-first and twenty-second chapters of the last book of the Bible, but I just couldn't do it!"

And this is the heaven that God has prepared for you

and for me and for the least of us that believe on Him.

Heaven will be a place of high and noble companionship. "And I say unto you, That many shall come from the east and from the west, and shall sit down with Abraham, and Isaac, and Jacob, in the kingdom of heaven" (Matt. 8:11). All the purest, most unselfish, dedicated men and women the world has ever known, all who in simple faith have trusted in the vicarious death and the atoning blood of Jesus Christ, will be there. All our dear ones who believed in and loved our Lord will be there. And best of all, the Lord Jesus will be there. We shall never get tired of looking at Him.

Will we know our loved ones? Of course we will! On the Mount of Transfiguration the disciples immediately knew Moses and Elijah, though they had never seen them before. "For now we see through a glass, darkly; but then face to face; now I know in part; but then shall I know even as also I am known" (I Cor. 13:12).

Heaven will be a place that is free from everything that curses and mars our lives. The wisdom, the grace, the power of God assures and insures its perfections. In John's description of heaven he cannot find words to tell us of the things that we have not seen, so he tells us of those things that will not be there. To describe the positive side of heaven would stagger and overwhelm our most fanciful excursions of imagination. It would be just as difficult as it would be to tell an unborn child about the world it was soon to enter when it has known only the mother's womb. So John speaks negatively and tells us there will be no grinding toil, no heavy burdens, no disappointments, no discouragement, no sorrow. "Earth has no sorrow that heaven cannot heal." No suffering, no pain, no funeral processions, no separations, no tears. No heartbreaking moment when a coffin is lowered into the earth.

"I heard a great voice out of heaven saying, Behold, the tabernacle of God is with men, and he will dwell with them, and they shall be his people, and God himself shall be with them, and be their God."

"And God shall wipe away all tears from their eyes; and there shall be no more death, neither sorrow, nor crying, neither shall there be any more pain: for the former things are passed away" (Rev. 21:3-4).

It is small wonder that those who have seen the vision of it by faith are longingly homesick for the land of endless day. Paul, after a glimpse of heaven, longed to depart and be with Christ, which he said was far better.

Men have dreamed of Utopias, envisioned the perfection of our earthly state, only to fail in miserable defeat because of man's innate weakness, sinfulness and inadequate resources. It is only in that glory land that these joys and lofty dreams will find their fulfillment. There, and only there, will the fatherhood of God and the brotherhood of man come to realization. The hell of war will be over. The ravaging power of sin will be ended forever. The separating power of death will be swallowed up in a final total victory.

Heaven is an eternal place. Nineveh, Carthage, Babylon, Greece, the former glory of Rome, etc., are gone and the wild beasts roam where once their temples stood. Heaven is a city whose builder and maker is God and the foundation will never crumble away. "For here we have no continuing city, but we seek one to come" (Heb. 13:14). Its splendor will be forever unchanged for two reasons:

(1) The attacks of Satan upon all that is good and holy will be over. Satan transformed the blossoming Eden into a poisonous wilderness. He robbed man of his Edenic innocence and put enmity between man and God. With this victory to encourage him, Satan wrought disease and disaster without resistance for thousands of years and was daring enough to challenge the "Lion of the tribe of Judah." But after forty days of continuous struggle, he met defeat in the Judean wilderness. He could not conquer the King of kings! All hell tried but failed in its attack upon Him.

(2) The splendor of heaven will exist forever because there will be no decay, none of the ravages of time. "The world and all its passionate desires will one day disappear. But the man who is following God's will is part of the permanent and cannot die" (I John 2:17, Phillips). When the sun is burned out and the stars have turned to ashes and drifted from their place in the sky, we shall be but beginning our eternal life in the presence of our Saviour—personally, consciously and forever.

Heaven will be a place of intellectual activity. Sir Isaac Newton, with his profound mind, has long ago stopped "picking up pebbles," and has gone down to the very bottom of the unexplored ocean of truth.

Our faculties will be intensified and all the pages of knowledge will unroll before us. God will touch our dull minds with intellectual acumen so that we will be able to grapple with the infinite mysteries of the universe.

There will be nothing in heaven to cause separation. We shall constantly enjoy each other's companionship in the presence of the One above all others, the One who makes it heaven — the Lord Jesus Christ.

What assurance we have in the promise of our Lord: "I am the resurrection and the life: he that believeth in me, though he were dead, yet shall he live" (John 11:25). We who have trusted our souls to the risen, living Christ, can affirm with Peter: "Blessed be the God and Father of our Lord Jesus Christ, which according to His abundant mercy hath begotten us again unto a lively hope by the resurrection of Jesus Christ from the dead, To an inheritance incorruptible, and undefiled, that fadeth not away, reserved in heaven for you, Who are kept by the power of God through faith unto salvation ready to be revealed in the last time" (I Peter 1:3-5). By the incarnation, the matchless life, the ignominious death, the shed blood, the glorious resurrection, the truth of the ascension, the Word of God, the testimony of the Holy Spirit, we are secure. Christ died to pave the way to heaven for those who believe in Him. So death is simply a transition, the opening of a gateway through the merits of our Saviour into a richer, fuller, more abundant life.

I know not where His islands lift
Their fronded palms in air;

I only know I cannot drift
Beyond His love and care.
I know not what the future hath
Of marvel or surprise,
Assured alone that life and death
His mercy underlies.

In the old days the sailors used to greet each other with the words, "What cheer?" An old pilot lay on his death bed. He had held a pilot's commission for nearly forty years and for almost all of those years he had been an earnest follower of Jesus Christ. A fellow seaman came to see him during his illness and would greet him with the words, "What cheer?"

The old pilot would answer, "The homeland heaves in sight."

Then one morning, in answer to the question, "What cheer?" he feebly responded, "Rounding the cape, almost in."

The family thought his mind was wandering and that in his delirium he was out on the sea; but in the late afternoon, as they put the question once more, "What cheer?" the old pilot said with a quivering lip, "In the port; let the anchor go." And at that moment the anchor was slipped and the old seaman was "in the port," Home at last and Home to stay. Home!

Just think
Of stepping on shore,
And finding it heaven;
Of taking hold of a hand,
And finding it God's hand;

Of breathing new air,
    And finding it celestial air;
Of feeling invigorated,
    and finding it immortality;
Of passing from storm and
    tempest to an unbroken calm;
Of waking up—
    And finding it Home.

Perhaps the sweetest description of heaven is found in John 17:24, "Father, I will that they also, whom thou hast given me, be with me where I am; that they may behold my glory, which thou hast given me: for thou lovest me before the foundation of the world."

Where Jesus is, 'tis Heaven there!

chapter nine

THE CROWNING PROOF
OF IMMORTALITY

Read Matthew 27:57; 28:1-20

"I am the resurrection, and the life: he that believeth in me, though he were dead, yet shall he live: And whosoever liveth and believeth in me shall never die" (John 11:25,26).

" . . . . because I live ye shall live also" (John 14:19).

" . . . Fear not; I am the first and the last: I am he that liveth, and was dead; and, behold, I am alive forevermore, Amen; and have the keys of hell and of death" (Rev. 1:17,18).

The supreme evidence of the fact of everlasting life and the truth of immortality is the resurrection of Jesus Christ from the dead. This is indeed the crowning proof. Early in His ministry the Lord Jesus Christ offered this as the great supernatural sign to the nations to demonstrate His deity. When the critics of His day asked, "What sign showest thou?" the Saviour replied, "An evil and adulterous generation seeketh after a sign; and there shall be no sign given to it, but the sign of the prophet

Jonas: For as Jonas was three days and three nights in the whale's belly; so shall the Son of Man be three days and three nights in the heart of the earth" (Matt. 12:39,40).

Because only God can save from sin and because salvation is inherent in our faith in the deity of Jesus Christ, the tenth chapter of Romans firmly teaches that belief in the literal resurrection of our Lord is an essential to salvation: "If thou shalt confess with thy mouth the Lord Jesus, and shalt believe in thine heart that God hath raised Him from the dead, thou shalt be saved" (Rom. 10:9).

Since the resurrection is a sign of the deity of Jesus Christ, acceptance of that sign is a confession of faith that He who is our Saviour is God and thus able to save. The resurrection of Jesus Christ is the solid foundation upon which the reality of our own resurrection is firmly established. In I Corinthians 15, Paul, following the reasoning of the Holy Spirit, says that if Christ did not rise from the dead, then we will not be raised. But if He was in truth raised from the dead, then our resurrection is as certain to be as His was an accomplished fact.

In Acts 17:31 the resurrection of Christ is presented to the Gentile nations as proof that God will receive and forgive all those who turn to Him through faith in His Son.

No event in history has been as well-authenticated and established as the resurrection of Jesus Christ. If over five hundred reliable eye witnesses were to testify unanimously in a case before a modern court, that court unhesitatingly would accept the testimony of the witnesses as truth. More than five hundred reliable witnesses saw Jesus Christ alive in a body of flesh and bone after His resurrection from the dead.

Thirty thousands male Jews of military age were crucified around the walls of Jerusalem by Titus and Pontius Pilate. Although approximately the average age of Jesus when He died, and crucified on Roman crosses during the same brief period of time, no student of history can name one of the thirty thousand.

How can we account for the fact that all the other martyred Jews remained nameless, while the whole world remembers the name of one? The simple explanation must be that all but one remained dead, and the dead are soon forgotten. This alone would establish the resurrection of the Lord Jesus to have been a literal, historical occurrence. So we can reasonably base our hope for immortality upon this historical, irrefutable, demonstrated fact.

Robert Burns, the Scottish poet, was walking down the street one day in Edinburgh and stopped to look in a window at a dramatic painting of the crucifixion. He noticed a small, ragged boy beside him and addressing him said, "What is that picture?"

"Don't you really know? That's the Roman soldiers killing Jesus," replied the little lad. The poet started on his way without further comment and had gone just a short distance when he felt a tug on his coat and turning he saw his little friend, who said, breathlessly: "Excuse me, Sir, but I forgot to tell you the most wonderful part of the story: He rose from the dead!"

The resurrection is literally the crux of Christianity and is one of the most definite, most repeated assurances of divine revelation.

Recent excavations have uncovered the extended tombs of the kings of Ur of the Chaldees, and have shown us that at the death of the ruler his entire court was buried alive. In Egypt the tomb of Tutankhamen, with its lavish wealth and artistic adornment, has impressed even our age. In the Red Square in Moscow the remains of the Red dictator, Lenin, preserved by a mysterious process, are regarded with an admiration that approaches worship. But we Christians point to a vacant tomb and a living, resurrected Christ.

We actually know more about the burial of Jesus Christ than any character in ancient history — king of Babylon, philosopher of Greece or triumphant Caesar. We know the tomb in which His body was placed, and the name of the man who owned it — Joseph of Arimathaea. We know a stone was rolled against the tomb, and that at the Jews' request Roman guards were set before it to prevent the body from being stolen. We know there is absolutely no question about that tomb in Joseph's garden being empty on the morning of the third day. No infidel, agnostic, atheist or unbeliever has ever been able to explain the empty tomb. If a single particle of bone were found that could be attributed to Jesus, the Christian structure would crumble. That empty tomb has been the most fascinating truth of the centuries. This fact alone should establish the resurrection of Jesus Christ to have been a literal, historical occurrence.

However, let us look at some of the theories that unbelievers have advanced in their effort to get rid of the crowning proof of immortality — the resurrection of the Lord Jesus Christ. There are many of them but basically only three:

(1) Some say the disciples stole Jesus' body and then deliberately tried to deceive the world. "They gave large money unto the soldiers, Saying, Say ye, His disciples came by night, and stole him away while we slept" (Matt. 28:12,13). I suppose this was the first rationalistic explanation of the resurrection. Let us consider the situation.

Why should these plotting disciples, these so-called villainous conspirators, want to take away the body of Jesus? If Christ had been buried in the potter's field, they might want to claim His body and put it in a better place. But when a wealthy aristocrat offered the poor, bruised body a beautiful home, why should they want to take it away? In the first place, they could not get at the body. In the second place, what would they have done with it? In the third place, how could they go out to preach the Gospel of the resurrection — fight for it and die for it — when they knew it was founded upon a lie? Men die for many things — for God, for home, their native land, but they do not die for what they know to be a lie. Christianity is not founded on a ghoulish graveyard robbery. Western civilization was not built on an ancient lie. Truth will out sooner or later and a lie does not live 2,000 years, especially when it is constantly being searched out. "This must be acknowledged, that Jesus has risen."

(2) Some say He never died: He was merely in a

swoon and that the odor of the spices and the cool air of the tomb revived Him; that He got up and left the tomb, rejoined His disciples and lived and died a natural death. This theory raises more difficulties than the miracle it attempts to explain. By the time of the resurrection Jesus had been dead for something like forty hours. The record states that when the soldiers came to Jesus and the thieves on the cross, the difference between Jesus and the thieves was a very obvious one — Jesus was dead; but the thieves were not yet dead and so their legs were broken. We are told, "The soldiers . . . brake not His (Jesus') legs" (John 19:32,33). The record also states that a soldier pierced Jesus' side with his spear and there came forth blood and water. That one wound fully proved the death of Jesus. The water flowing through the wound indicated that the spear had penetrated the pericardium in which that water was lodged; and the wound must necessarily have brought death immediately.

Pilate made careful inquiry and learned that Jesus was dead before he ever granted Joseph of Arimathaea permission to take the body down from the cross. David Strauss was right when he said, "A man who crept forth and crawled about, a fit subject for a hospital, could never have so impressed His disciples that He was the conqueror of death and the grave as to have made their moral transformation one of the marvels of the world." If this theory were true, the disciples were fools or liars.

They recorded all sorts of things about our Lord after His resurrection that could not be true of Him if He came out of the tomb with the same physical body He had when He entered. This theory would make our

Lord unworthy. Do you suppose that for one moment the Lord Jesus Christ would risk the founding of Christianity, which He expected to sweep around the world and which He knew would arouse the keenest antagonism of those hardened Jews; risk the criticism of Gentile philosophers and the challenge of the dictum of science, upon a statement so flimsy and so easy to be discredited as this? What an unprincipled monster the Lord Jesus Christ would be to convince His disciples that He had died when He had not. Was this deception the power that was to convert the world and furnish the ground of their hope? Would they lay down their lives for a lie? The claims that He made revealed Him to be the Son of God and there was no sin in Him, let alone the despicable sin of chicanery, fraud, and outright deceit. Contemporary Roman historians Tacitus, Josephus, and Pliny record His death. The swoon conjecture is impossible and incredible.

(3) Others say the disciples had a brain storm. They were hallucinated. This is the famous vision theory. Joseph Ernest Renan and Strauss were the outstanding proponents of this theory. "A hallucinated woman gave the world a resurrected God!" The claim is that the hallucination was built on expectancy, but the theory collapses because, if the Gospel makes anything plain, it is that the resurrection was the one thing that they were *not* expecting. When He did appear the Scripture says, "They were terrified and affrighted, and supposed that they had seen a spirit" (Luke 24:37). This is proof that they never expected to see Him; and because they did not expect to see Him, the idea that they were

hallucinated has no basis. They had difficulty believing what they saw. Our Lord had to labor to convince them that He had actually risen. "Afterward he appeared unto the eleven as they sat at meat, and upbraided them with their unbelief and hardness of heart, because they believed not them which had seen him after he was risen" (Mark 16:14). The truth of our Lord's resurrection was obviously not hysteria but history.

The evidences of the resurrection are so overwhelming that it is impossible to sift through them thoroughly and come to any other conclusion than that Christ did literally and physically rise from the dead on the morning of that third day as He said He would. Our Lord promised that though they might destroy the temple of His body, He would raise it up again three days later. He declared that this experience was prefigured in the sign of Jonah: "For as Jonas was three days and three nights in the whale's belly; so shall the Son of Man be three days and three nights in the heart of the earth" (Matt. 12:40).

The resurrection of Christ was predicted in the old Testament. Psalm 16:10 declares that Christ, God's Holy One, shall not be left in death and shall not see corruption.

Then there is the triumphant cry of victory by the palsied Job as he looked toward the hidden future: "For I know that my redeemer liveth, and that he shall stand at the latter day upon the earth: And though after my skin worms destroy this body, yet in my flesh shall I see God" (Job 19:25,26). Verbally inspired by God, these prophecies are so powerful and compelling that even if the later records disappeared or were destroyed, they would give us the assurance that our blessed Saviour, having been "cut off out of the land of the living," would nevertheless "prolong his days," to use the very words with which Isaiah anticipated His resurrection (Isa. 53).

Today we sentence a man to death on circumstantial evidence. But the enemies of Christ are determined not to let Jesus live, even though the testimony for His resurrection is overwhelming. One evidence is seen in the duty that was given to the guards. After Jesus was crucified under the careful supervision of experienced Roman legionnaires, the hands of Joseph of Arimathaea laid Him away in an impregnable tomb. A mammoth stone was rolled before the sepulchre and secured with the seal of Rome. Soldiers with spears bristling stood before the tomb night and day to guard the body of a dead man. Why? The answer is proof of the resurrection. "Now the next day, that followed the day of the preparation, the chief priests and Pharisees came together unto Pilate, Saying, Sir, we remember that that deceiver said, while He was yet alive, After three days I will rise again. Command therefore that the sepulchre be made sure until the third day, lest his disciples come by night, and steal Him away, and say unto the people, He is risen from the dead: so that the last error shall be worse than the first" (Matt. 27:62-64).

Every precaution was taken to secure that tomb. The religious leaders of the day should have known, from the study of the prophets and from the evidence of darkness, earthquakes and other supernatural phenomena that accompanied the death of our Lord Jesus Christ, something unnatural was taking place and that they had crucified God in the flesh. The fact that they sealed the tomb and set a guard was an unconscious confession that in their hearts they questioned as to whether they had indeed crucified Deity. Otherwise what idiocy was this that the Roman government would send strong, brave men to keep a dead man from walking away? All the power of Rome was back of the seal that was placed upon that grave, and let me assure you that all the power of Satan and hell was present to keep that body within the death chamber. When we read that the keepers of the tomb fell back as dead men, we know that nothing short of divine power could produce such an effect. When Rome sent soldiers to watch the tomb, they removed all possibility of the resurrection of Christ being a farce and left an assurance for all ages that the resurrection of Jesus Christ was an incontrovertible reality.

Two days after He was first placed in the tomb, the Pharisees nervously, anxiously awaited the issue. Hour after hour rolled by and all was still. But on the morning of the third day He illuminated the dark enclosure of the tomb with His resurrection glory. He burst the bands of death, broke the Roman seal, and came forth the conqueror of death, the grave, and hell itself. The very fact that the Roman guard lived to tell their story is proof that they did not fall asleep while on guard duty at the tomb. If they had, they would have been executed. The obvious fact is that a crooked bargain had been made in an attempt to cover up the resurrection. Today the tomb in Joseph's garden is still empty.

The Mohammedans make pilgrimages to Medina where

the dust of the prophet Mohammed lies. The Buddhists have a temple in which they keep the last remains of Buddha — a single tooth. If the body of Jesus had been found even in the first hundred years, the New Testament would never have been written. The fact of the resurrection was the basis of Peter's great message on the day of Pentecost. As was prophesied, the body of our Lord never saw corruption. Christ's resurrection had more than five hundred witnesses (I Cor. 15:6).

Certain institutions and conditions exist in our day that are effects. Millions of Christians are worshipping on the first day of the week rather than on the Jewish Sabbath. To distinguish themselves from the Jews (to whom Christ is dead and who still look for a Messiah who has not come) the people of God worship Jesus Christ on the day He rose from the dead, which testifies to the fact of a living Christ. As Christians we commemorate the resurrection of Christ. In the experience of the Christian church every Lord's Day is Easter!

Consider the Christian church. It is an effect. What was the cause? If Jesus did not rise from the dead bodily, physically, there would be no church. During the centuries a handful of disciples has grown into an institution with some nine hundred million members. Their presence in the world is a testimony to the fact that their Founder rose from the dead.

Consider the New Testament. It is an effect of Christ's resurrection. If Jesus had remained buried, the story of His life and death would have remained buried with Him, and there would be nothing to write about.

Consider the change in the disciples. At Calvary they

forsook Him and fled, because they thought it was all over. See the same disciples a few weeks later at Pentecost. Peter, standing in the midst of those who consented to the murder of the Son of God, boldly accusing them: "Therefore let all the house of Israel know assuredly, that God hath made that same Jesus, whom ye have crucified, both Lord and Christ" (Acts 2:36). What changed these timid disciples into fearless witnesses, counting it a privilege to suffer for the name of the Lord Jesus Christ, to give their lives for the Gospel? It was the fact that they saw Jesus alive after His resurrection and nothing was ever the same again. They did not fear death.

Every true disciple of Christ has in his own life a witness to the resurrection of Jesus Christ. Consider the conversion of the Apostle Paul, how he endured poverty, strife, hunger, imprisonment, and finally a gruesome death. He wrote fourteen epistles unexcelled in literature. His end was a Roman dungeon, an executioner's ax. Would imagination, nightmare, or spirit visitant carry a man through these life-and-death trials? He saw the Lord Jesus Christ, and his life was revolutionized.

Paul believed the story of the empty tomb at a date when the recollection was fresh, when he could examine the evidence for himself, when he could make the fullest possible inquiry. His conclusion was, "I delivered unto you first of all that which I also received, how that Christ died for our sins according to the scriptures; and that he was buried, and that he rose again the third day according to the scriptures" (I Cor. 15:3,4). The stars are not looking down upon a tomb in Palestine where a decayed and corrupted body speaks to us as only a memory, because Christ is alive and death has lost its sting forever for those who put their trust in Him.

Christ's resurrection furnished every believer with a God-given assurance that he is justified in Christ. His resurrection was the seal of His redemptive work. It was the indication that what He had finished was accepted of the Father. The fact that Christ rose was evidence that the Father was satisfied with His sacrifice. His resurrection was a receipt for a finished transaction and the cross is explained only by the resurrection. The debt was paid on Calvary, but it was receipted on the morning of the third day. He was delivered for our offenses, and was raised again for our justification (Romans 4:25).

The resurrection is the pledge of His future triumph. The disciples expected Him to establish a literal kingdom. They overlooked the fact of His suffering, because they were looking for His glory. But they were not entirely mistaken: He *is* to have a literal kingdom on this earth one day. Otherwise He would never be vindicated in the world where He endured shame. The resurrection of Jesus Christ assures us of this ultimate triumph that one day He will come again. It assures us that we have a personal Saviour who, with a flesh and bone body, is seated at the right hand of the Father, as our advocate and representative. He is a living companion who promised, " . . . I am with you alway . . . " (Matt. 28:20). His presence can save us from sin and its wages; He can give us light for darkness in our dying hour, and He can show us the abundant and joy-crowned life. No one can ever take us from Christ. There is no night, no darkness, no farewell in heaven. We are Christ's forever.

Jesus' resurrection robs death of its sting. We can even learn to welcome death and in the spirit of the Christian martyrs, who rejoiced that they would soon behold their Lord, conquer the fear of the "last enemy," through the love of Christ. God always heals a believer. Sometimes He does it through the marvelous skill of medicine; sometimes He does it through the skill of surgery; sometimes He does it through the insight and aid of a trained, competent counselor, particularly when the seat of our illness is in the area of a disturbed mind; sometimes He does it instantly and miraculously by the power of His Holy Spirit; but always He does it in the morning of the resurrection. *He never fails us.* We who know Him can defy Satan, the grave and hell with this powerful cry of victory: "O death, where is thy sting? O grave, where is thy victory? The sting of death is sin; and the strength of sin is the law. But thanks be to God, which giveth us the victory through our Lord Jesus Christ" (I Cor. 15:55-57).

In the light of His resurrection we can tell the Christian mother that she will again see the little babe that she has laid to rest. We can tell the mothers and fathers who wake at midnight and think of their Christian sons who have died on far-flung battlefields or who have been buried at sea, that though they have fallen, they will see them again.

His resurrection assures us of our own resurrection. This truth assures us that our bodies will be resurrected. Our Lord had a body with physically identifiable characteristics, but with none of the limitations of our physical world. He was no apparition. He built a fire; He cooked fish and He ate. Clearly the Apostle writes in those faith-sustaining words of I Corinthians 15:42,43 that the Christian's body "is sown in corruption; it is raised in incorruption . . . it is sown in weakness; it is raised in power." If God created our bodies for life on earth, can He not recreate them for life in heaven? If the grave could not hold Him, it cannot hold us. He is the first fruits, and the believers who will be raised at His coming will be the harvest, the full fruit. Our Lord's resurrection body is a pattern of ours. He has a corporal body and so we shall have.

On a tombstone in Philadelphia appears the following inscription:

> The body of Benjamin Franklin, printer, like the cover of an old book, its contents torn out and stripped of lettering and gilding, lies here food for worms. But the works shall not be lost, for it will appear once more in a new and more elegant edition, revised and corrected by its Author.

His resurrection is a guarantee that we shall see Him one day face to face. "Beloved, now are we the sons of God, and it doth not yet appear what we shall be: but we know that, when he shall appear, we shall be like him; for we shall see him as he is" (I John 3:2). In eternity we shall rejoice in the glorious privilege of expressing adoration for our crucified, living Saviour.

Christ's resurrection is the guarantee of personal victory over sin. Since Christ is risen, we need not be slaves to sin, nor subject to the bondage of Satan. Because He has risen, we may walk in newness of life, more than conquerors through Him Who loved us and gave Himself for us. This certainty of the resurrection gives reality to the proclamation of the Gospel. It gives substance to our faith, power to our testimony, certainty to our salvation, joy to our lives, success to our service, puts the seal of authority on every claim of Christ, and guarantees the realization of every Biblical hope that dwells in the soul of a believer.

We are told that on Mars Hill the Apostle Paul preached the resurrection to the Greeks. "He (God) hath appointed a day, in the which he will judge the world in righteousness by that man whom he hath ordained; whereof he hath given assurance unto all men, in that he hath raised him from the dead. And when they heard of the resurrection of the dead, some mocked: and others said, We will hear thee again of this matter. So Paul departed from among them. Howbeit certain men clave unto him, and believed . . . " (Acts 17:31-34).

There were three reactions to Paul's sermon on the resurrection. The pattern of these responses is in evidence every time the Gospel message is proclaimed. There were the unbelievers who mocked. There were the indecisive procrastinators who said, "We will hear thee again of this matter." They postponed their decision and deferred accepting Christ. That is why the Word of God urges us through the Holy Spirit that " . . . now is the accepted time; behold now is the day of salvation" (II Cor. 6:2).

The third group in the Apostle's audience consisted of those who "clave unto him, and believed." There on Mars Hill the Spirit of God touched their hearts and they were saved. What a thought it is! If you do not allow this claim of Christ upon your life, He might as well be sealed up in a dusty vault in Palestine and forever dead.

The captain of a transatlantic liner related that many years ago one of his passengers was the talented young singer, Jenny Lind, whose beautiful voice was dedicated to the service of the Lord Jesus Christ. He said that one morning she arose early, undoubtedly for the purpose of standing on the bridge to watch the sun rise out of the trackless ocean. The radiance of daybreak evidently awoke within her heart the thought of eternity and she began to sing from Handel's *Messiah* that unforgettable passage beginning, "I know that my Redeemer liveth," climaxing with the great triumphant words: "I, too, shall live!" The captain of the ocean vessel said it was one of the most exalted moments of his life.

If you can greet each new day with the song of resurrection triumph, if you can say in the depths of your soul, "I know that my Redeemer liveth," you can end all life's days with the Christ-centered confidence, "I, too, shall live!"